Summary
and Note-Taking

Revised Edition

Previously published by Georgian Press

Marian Barry

CAMBRIDGE
UNIVERSITY PRESS

University Printing House, Cambridge CB2 8BS, United Kingdom

One Liberty Plaza, 20th Floor, New York, NY 10006, USA

477 Williamstown Road, Port Melbourne, VIC 3207, Australia

4843/24, 2nd Floor, Ansari Road, Daryaganj, Delhi – 110002, India

79 Anson Road, #06–04/06, Singapore 079906

Cambridge University Press is part of the University of Cambridge.

It furthers the University's mission by disseminating knowledge in the pursuit of education, learning and research at the highest international levels of excellence.

Information on this title: education.cambridge.org

First published by Georgian Press (Jersey) Limited 2004
Second edition 2006
Reprinted and published by Cambridge University Press 2010
20 19 18 17 16 15 14 13

Printed in the United Kingdom by Latimer Trend

A catalogue record for this publication is available from the British Library

ISBN 978-0-521-14092-8 Paperback without key
ISBN 978-0-521-14094-2 Paperback with key

Produced by AMR Design Ltd (www.amrdesign.com)

CONTENTS

This book provides summary and note-taking practice for the revised (2006) syllabus of the Cambridge IGCSE examination in English as a Second Language (Papers 1 and 2). By developing and improving note-taking and summarising skills in general, the exercises will also be helpful for studies across the curriculum, and for preparation for the demands of academic reading and writing at higher levels.

By working through the exercises, students should improve their ability to:

- analyse typical IGCSE-style questions
- read and understand the usual kinds of texts set in the exam
- extract key information from texts
- present information clearly and logically
- write better-connected prose.

Organisation and themes

There are six theme-based sections, each containing exam-format summary and note-taking exercises. These include 'linked summary' exercises, in which students produce a short summary based on their notes.

The themes and texts have been chosen for their appeal to young people, for their applicability to international contexts, and because they are similar in type, level of complexity and length to those found in the actual exam. The first section, for example, focuses on the impact of science on society and explores a range of health-related issues. The texts are from popular magazines and newspapers and require no specialised scientific knowledge.

Examiner's tips

The examiner's tips throughout the book give practical advice on the exam itself. They also help build learner independence by developing self-help learning strategies, and include suggestions for language development outside the classroom.

Using the material in the classroom

Although the summary and note-taking exercises make convenient practice tests or homework exercises, it is worth using many of the texts for learning in the classroom. Classroom teaching and support can be reduced as students progress through the book, leaving selected exercises to be done under exam conditions as part of a mock exam. Alternatively, periodic tests can be set to measure progress.

Preparing for reading

It is a good idea to prepare students for the reading texts, rather than asking them to plunge straight in. For issue-based texts, for example, you could write a sentence on the board such as 'This class believes that children should be vaccinated against smoking' and then elicit views on the advantages and disadvantages of such a policy.

Students can be asked to predict the content of a text by discussing what they can glean from information in the heading and any accompanying picture. You can also write questions on the board for students to find the answers to as they read. The questions can be fairly straightforward, such as (for the text on page 34) 'Where in Australia did Louise get lost?' or 'Who were the first people Louise met after her escape?'

Analysing the question

Students can be guided and supported, especially in the early stages, in analysing the question itself. You may wish to write the question on the board, for instance, and ask a student to come forward and underline the key words. This can lead to a useful discussion as to whether these are, in fact, they 'key' words, and, if not, why.

Reading the text

Reading can be done silently, or by students taking turns aloud. Remind them that careful reading is vital for good comprehension of the text, as without it they can easily miss or lose track of the essential detail. After reading, you may like to elicit views on the context of the text, or draw attention to a particular language construction or item of vocabulary. Students can then be asked to carry out the summary or note-taking task itself.

Feedback and common mistakes

It is helpful to give students feedback on completed exercises, as well as a mark. You may notice that the same sorts of errors have been made by several students. Completed answers (perhaps an amalgam of work from various students) could be reproduced on the board or an OHP, and you might then like to elicit views as to why answers are correct or not.

Common mistakes you may wish to highlight include:

- putting the correct piece of information under the wrong heading
- giving an incomplete answer, with a vital bit of information missing
- giving an answer which is too general, rather than specific
- copying a true fact from the text which has no relevance to the actual question asked.

It is also encouraging to show good examples of students' answers and to elicit from the class the reasons for their success.

Helping students to improve their summaries

To help students to improve their summary writing, you could select from their work examples which have a particular weakness and ask for suggestions for improvement. Problematic areas might be grammar, linking words, punctuation, spelling, irrelevance, repetition, little attempt to use own words, or redundant language. For example, you might choose a paragraph which has the correct content points in short, simple sentences but which does not flow well. You could ask: *'How could these two sentences be joined together?'* (eliciting linking words), *'What could make this sentence more interesting?'* (eliciting an introductory phrase), or *'This sentence is copied from the text. How could we put it into our own words?'*

Summaries are usually focused on one topic, which leads some students to start each sentence with exactly the same word – for example, with the word *Dogs* in a summary about dogs. To show

them how to avoid this, pick out a sentence and ask how it could start differently. For example, *'Dogs should not be allowed to jump on furniture'* could be altered to *'Jumping on furniture should not be allowed'*. Ask students if the meaning is the same or different. Then discuss whether other structures are possible. Students may produce *'Don't allow dogs to jump on furniture'*. You could offer clue words such as *Don't* to help less able students.

Make sure students understand that a summary with a monotonous structure is not grammatically wrong, but that variety in the way sentences are organised is better style. They should be encouraged to think of the way the whole paragraph flows, and to use connectors and complex clauses, rather than simply concentrating on individual sentences.

Note-taking for Core level

In the exam, eight marks are allocated for note-taking on Paper 2 (Extended) and six for Paper 1 (Core). The exercises in this book follow the Extended-level format, requiring students to find information for each of eight bullet points. To help Core-level students, you could ask them to find only six points, giving them the answers for the two 'spare' bullet points, or eliciting these before they start the exercise.

Linked summaries

The linked summary exercises, based on the preceding note-taking, provide ideal practice for Paper 1, in which Core-level students produce a paragraph based on an aspect or aspects of the notes they have already written. They are very suitable for differentiated classroom work or homework, as they support and guide students into producing a summary. While they are of particular value to students achieving at the lower end of the range, they can also be a useful confidence builder for more able students. It is a good idea to check that the preceding note-taking exercise has been correctly completed before students begin, to ensure everyone is starting off on the right path.

Marking summary questions

The marks for Extended-level summaries are divided into six for content and four for the ability to write good, connected prose. The answer key sometimes lists more than six possible content points. Explain to students that once they are sure they have found six points that cover all aspects of the question, they should stop looking for further points. Detailed guidelines for marking the language aspect of the summary questions are given on page 90.

The linked summary is marked out of four for language ability only, not content. However, if the content is completely irrelevant, no marks would be awarded.

Slashes and brackets in the answer key

The same point from a text can often be expressed in a variety of ways. If this is the case, slashes are used in the answer key to show paraphrasing of the same idea. Brackets are used to show how a correct point may be extended or elaborated. However, the information in the brackets is optional – a student does not need to give this information or order to get full marks.

Model answers

Model answers for all summary and linked summary questions are provided in the answer key, and are of the appropriate length (up to 100 words or 70 words respectively). Examiners do not use model answers when marking, but they are included here as examples of how connected prose can be structured to provide suitable exam-style answers.

Topic vocabulary

In the topic vocabulary lists on pages 57–80, lexical items selected from the texts are loosely organised into groups, providing a valuable and flexible resource. Collocations and phrases are included, as well as individual words. Space is provided for students to write notes and translations, if they wish, and to add further words to each group. Suggestions for using the vocabulary in the classroom are given on page 56.

Topic-related writing tasks

Exam-style writing tasks based on the topics in the summary and note-taking exercises are provided on pages 82–88. These are cross-referenced to the appropriate topic vocabulary lists, to encourage students to select relevant vocabulary to help them.

You may like to discuss the writing task before students begin, to make sure everyone understands what is required, drawing attention to the tone and register needed for the stated audience. Encourage students to identify the most suitable words and phrases from the topic vocabulary list. You could list these and others on the board, then select some examples and elicit how they might fit into complete sentences. This approach will help students make a really positive beginning with essay writing, as the most difficult part is starting off. By recycling topic vocabulary appropriately in work of their own, they will improve their grasp of how it works in context, and will have genuinely broadened their vocabularies.

A tried and tested method for writing summaries and notes

Here is a tried and tested method for writing notes and summaries, which has been used successfully by many students. You may, of course, work out your own preferred method.

To approach a summary exercise

1 Read the question carefully and underline the key words as you read.
2 Look carefully at the heading, and at any pictorial information, such as a photograph or diagram, in order to pick up extra clues about the content before you begin to read the text.
3 Read the text fairly quickly, with as much concentration as possible. Slow down and re-read any parts you find confusing.
4 Underline key parts of the text that are relevant to the question.
5 Draft a rough paragraph from the key words and phrases, using sentences. Use your own words as far as you can. Specialised terms and technical words do **not** need to be changed, however.
6 Count the number of words you have written. Make corrections to the grammar and spelling if necessary, and add any linking words to make your paragraph flow more smoothly.
7 Write a final draft in about 100 words (or no more than 70 words for the linked summary). If you find you do not have time to write out a neat final copy, making corrections to the first draft, such as altering punctuation, putting in a linking word or correcting grammar, is quite acceptable and well worth doing.

To approach a note-taking exercise

Use the above method as far as step **4**. Then complete any bullet points or numbered points by copying short, relevant words and phrases from the text, or using words of your own. You do **not** need to write complete sentences.

Be selective and don't just copy out large parts of the original. Remember, you are making notes, not writing paragraphs. Your completed notes should be brief, concise and easily understood, even by someone who has not seen the original text.

Time management

As you get closer to the exam, the amount of time you spend on the summary and note-taking exercises will become more crucial. Remember that Paper 1 is one-and-a-half hours long and contains seven questions. Paper 2 is two hours long and contains seven questions. Obviously, you will have to divide your time sensibly among all the questions on the Paper. It's a bad idea to spend too long on any particular question and then not have enough time to complete all the questions.

A good tip is to write down how long it takes you to produce a summary or note-taking exercise and then try to improve that time as you progress through your course. As a general rule, you should spend about 20 minutes on the summary exercise (or 10 minutes on the linked summary), and about 15 minutes on the note-taking exercise. Remember, though, that this has to include all the stages of the exercise, such as reading the question carefully, final checking and making last-minute improvements. These are very important and can make a big difference to your results.

Read the article describing advances in medical technology. Then write a summary explaining the aims behind the development of the technology, and the issues that need to be addressed if the gadgets are to be suitable for the home. Write about 100 words and use your own words as far as possible.

A DOCTOR IN THE HOUSE

Brushing your teeth twice a day should keep the dentist away. But if a group of scientific researchers have their wish, it will make the rest of your body healthy too. A toothbrush that checks blood sugar and bacteria while you brush is currently in development in the USA. It is one of many gadgets proposed by engineers and doctors at the Center for Future Health in New York – others include a pair of spectacles that help to jog your memory, and a home camera designed to check for cancer.

The devices seem fanciful, but the basic principles are simple. The gadgets should make it easy for people to detect illness long before it strikes and so seek treatment far earlier than normal. Instead of relying on hi-tech hospitals, the emphasis is shifted to the home and easy-to-use gadgets. In the long run, the technology may even prevent illness by encouraging us to lead healthier lives.

Intelligent bandages are a good example. Powerful sensors within the bandage could quickly identify tiny amounts of bacteria in a wound and determine which antibiotics would work best. The cut could then be treated instantly, so avoiding possible complications.

Socks are long overdue for a makeover. In the future they will be able to automatically detect the amount of pressure in your foot and alert you when an ulcer is imminent.

All the projects should have far-reaching implications, but the biggest single development is a melanoma monitor designed to give early warnings of cancer. The device could be used to take a picture of your body each week, then compare it to previous images. If a problem is found, the system would advise you to get a check-up at your doctor's surgery.

If all this sounds nerve-wracking, then help is at hand. Experts are also working on a 'digital doctor', complete with a comforting bedside manner. A standard computer would be able to understand your voice and answer questions about your symptoms in plain English and in a way which would calm your nerves.

Stress is no sweat either. A portable communication aid could recognise certain phrases and tones and let you know when you are about to lose your temper. The software would also suggest ways of keeping your cool.

Computer therapists are a little way off yet, but the projects are ready to be prototyped and trialled. Researchers are still struggling, however, with making the technology cheap and simple enough for the domestic user. That is going to be the difficult part.

....

....

....

....

....

....

....

....

....

....

....

....

....

....

....

....

Using linking words

EXAMINER'S TIP

When writing a summary, you often have to make a series of separate points. You can link them in different ways.

To build up a list of points, use linking words such as *firstly*, *secondly*, *also*, *in addition*, *as well as*, *furthermore* and *moreover*.

Linking words which show contrast include *but*, *although*, *on the other hand*, *in spite of*, *despite*, *however* and *nevertheless*.

Words for reasoning include *because*, *as*, *since*, and *for this reason*. Result or consequence can be expressed by *so*, *consequently*, *therefore* and *as a result*.

You can round off your argument or list of points with expressions like *Finally*, *On balance*, *To sum up* and *In conclusion*.

Apart from showing the examiner that you can reason and sequence your ideas clearly and logically, using linking words will also demonstrate that you are in control of sentence structure, and your paragraph will flow much better. This will help you to gain the highest marks.

Read the article about special hi-tech spectacles which are being adapted to help children suffering from dyslexia. Then write a set of notes, using the headings given.

TACKLING DYSLEXIA IN CHILDREN

Children who are dyslexic have problems processing specific visual information, resulting in trouble reading and writing. Until recently, it was thought to be language-related areas of the brain which were deficient, but new research suggests that dyslexics have difficulty with the control of eye movement, or 'eye wobble'.

Scientists based at the QuientiQ laboratory and researchers at the Dyslexia Research Trust are working together to adapt hi-tech spectacles, developed to monitor the eye movements of fighter pilots, into miniaturised versions for children as young as five.

It is hoped the technology will help children like the six-year-old boy who asked Dr Sue Fowler, a researcher at the Dyslexia Research Trust's clinic, 'Do you want to know a secret? All the words on the page move and I don't know how they do it because they don't have any legs.' Other children with dyslexia may report a disturbing sensation of 'glare' from the printed page, making them rub their eyes frequently. In some dyslexic children, reading causes a headache.

Professor John Stein, professor of neurology at Magdalene College, Oxford, has spent 20 years researching the connection between lack of eye control and reading difficulties. He says, 'We are visual animals and eye movements are possibly the most important movements we make because they allow us to inspect the world around us. I believe problems with eye wobble account for up to two-thirds of dyslexia cases.

'Dyslexia is not a disease. It is a brain difference, like left-handedness. We also believe that a cell in the brain, the magnocell, is related to eye movement. It seems that magnocells in dyslexics do not develop as well as those in good readers.'

The professor, who trained at Oxford and St Thomas's Hospital in London, will be meeting government officials to prepare for a trial of the hi-tech specs in primary schools in London and Hampshire. Professor Stein and his colleague, Dr Fowler, used the first prototype on a child last summer.

Professor Stein explains, 'Eye wobble is not obvious to the naked eye. The movements are small and very rapid. The hi-tech specs, which are worn for only a few minutes during tests, are the most accurate technique we have for detecting the amount of eye wobble. The child focuses on a point 18 inches away and then follows a moving target. The specs show whether the child's eyes are tracking steadily, or whether they wobble. We would like the specs to be mass-produced, becoming cheap enough to be used in all primary schools.'

Dr Fowler adds, 'We see 800 children a year from all over the country. They are mostly aged seven to twelve, but people of any age can be assessed. Because we are a charity and investigations are part of our research, children are seen free.

'If we can get children early, their brains are flexible enough to enable them to improve control. After seeing them at the clinic, we give patients daily exercises to enable them to keep their eyes still and fixed on one object. In time, we believe these exercises become etched onto the brain. The result is that reading improves greatly.'

Problems a dyslexic child may complain of

- ....
- ....
- ....
- ....

Original use of the hi-tech specs

- ....

How the specs are used to test children for dyslexia

- ....
- ....

Treatment after the tests

- ....

LINKED SUMMARY

Using the ideas in your notes, write a paragraph of no more than 70 words on the ways dyslexia may affect children, a technique for diagnosing dyslexia, and how dyslexia can be treated. Use your own words as far as possible.

Being aware of your reading speed

EXAMINER'S TIP

The speed at which students feel comfortable reading is a very personal matter and there is no doubt that individual speeds of reading vary hugely. Reading speed is not an indication of intelligence, although young people often believe it is.

The fact is, we all speed up and slow down as we read, depending on the difficulty of the content. We often do this quite unconsciously, whether we are reading for pleasure or reading for information. We sometimes read groups of words quite fast, taking in the information quickly and easily, without any conscious effort. You may be surprised by how quickly you 'get through' several chapters of an exciting novel. On the other hand, we naturally slow down or re-read a section of text when we want to be sure that we are getting the correct meaning from what we are reading.

Next time you read, you could try to be more aware of your reading speeds. When practising exam-style exercises, slow down a little if you begin to feel confused. Re-read a sentence or group of words, checking back with the question to see if this bit of text contains relevant information. Approaching your reading in this way is a more mature attitude to study than rushing through without understanding. Don't be worried about taking more time, as the few extra seconds of double-checking are definitely worth it.

Read the article about allergies. Then write a summary explaining why some people develop allergies, why allergic reactions seem to be increasing, and how medication can help. Write about 100 words and try to use your own words as far as possible.

THE ENEMY WITHIN

Allergy has become more and more common over the last 30 years. Now one-third of us are affected by allergy at some point in our lives and half of these sufferers are children. In the UK, three million people suffer from asthma, and five per cent of children suffer from food allergy.

Allergy is a reaction that occurs when the immune system has a strange and unnecessary reaction to a substance which is normally harmless, such as pollen or peanuts. The immune system is there to protect the body against outside attackers, including viruses, bacteria and parasites. To defend your body against an attacker, the immune system remembers these dangerous micro-organisms and attacks them if it meets them again. This work is done by antibodies. The immune system in allergy sufferers makes antibodies against harmless substances, because it mistakenly believes them to be dangerous.

An allergic reaction may not happen the first time a sufferer meets an allergen (the substance causing the reaction, such as pollen, milk or strawberries). Sometimes people can eat nuts for years and then suddenly become allergic to them. What has happened is that the immune system has now decided the substance is dangerous and has made an allergy antibody. This antibody then attaches itself to cells, which contain histamine. When the antibodies meet the allergen the next time, they attempt to destroy it. As they do that, the surface of the cells is broken, and histamine is released. The histamine and other chemicals inflame the tissues. This leads to the symptoms of allergy, such as swelling, rashes, sneezing, sore eyes and breathlessness. Anaphylaxia is the most severe allergic reaction of all and is most often triggered by wasp or bee stings or peanuts. This must be treated immediately.

Allergies run in families. Some people are born with the ability to make lots of allergy antibodies, and they are more likely to develop allergies and allergic disorders such as hay fever and asthma.

Experts believe more people have developed allergies because of changes in our lifestyle which have exposed us to more allergens. We eat more processed foods, with a wide range of additives and colourings; more and more people have central heating and double glazing, making our houses warmer and less draughty – an ideal environment to breed the house dust mite.

There may also be a link between allergies and antibiotics. At one time our immune systems were kept busy fighting off disease and trying to win the battle for health, but antibiotics have reduced the amount of work our immune systems have to do. Now experts think they may direct spare energy to harmless substances such as strawberries. In other words our immune systems have become over-sensitive.

A good deal of research is being devoted to finding a cure for allergies. Sufferers may be given medicine to control symptoms, and they may also be offered tests to find out what substances trigger an allergic reaction so that they can avoid contact with these in future.

....
....
....
....
....
....
....
....
....
....
....
....
....
....
....
....

Writing concisely

EXAMINER'S TIP

The summary question asks you to write 'about 100 words' – you are allowed to write a few words under or over 100. When practising summary writing, however, think about ways you can save yourself words.

For example, try not to copy out whole sentences from the text as this usually leads to using too many words. Also, several nouns in the text can often be grouped together as one collective noun, rather than listing each one separately. The collective noun you need may actually be in the text – for example, *allergen* on the opposite page, which can be used to refer to a list of substances such as *pollen*, *milk*, *strawberries*, *nuts*, etc. You have to decide yourself whether it is necessary to name each item separately in your summary, or whether it is possible to use the collective noun.

The advantages of using collective nouns are that, as well as reducing the number of words you write, they show the examiner that you have a good command of English.

Read the article about a vaccine to discourage cigarette smoking and complete the notes under the headings given.

STOP THEM BEFORE THEY START

Should every teenager be given a vaccine that blocks the effects of nicotine, and so prevents them becoming addicted to cigarettes?

This controversial possibility is on the horizon, thanks to the development of a new vaccine for nicotine addiction. The vaccine was designed for people who want to quit smoking but who repeatedly relapse after giving up. But since most countries are failing to cut the number of children and teenagers taking up smoking, many people will want to know whether the vaccine should be used far more widely if it proves to be effective.

The vaccine stimulates the immune system to produce antibodies against nicotine. When an antibody binds to nicotine, the resulting complex is too big to get into the brain, and so the brain's 'pleasure receptors' that give people enjoyment from smoking aren't activated.

'The vaccine will be tested first on relapsing smokers, then on those who plan to quit, then on those who are not yet completely hooked,' says Frank Vocci of the National Institute of Drug Abuse near Washington, DC, which sponsored the vaccine. 'The final step would be vaccinating young people before they even try smoking, but that's a long way down the road.'

John Roberts, medical director of British drugs company Xenova, is very enthusiastic. 'I think prevention is a huge opportunity,' he says. 'If you can take away the pleasure nicotine gives, then teenagers who start smoking are more likely to stop before it becomes a habit.' Future generations may thus avoid the serious health problems in midlife caused by smoking.

Eighty per cent of smokers start in their teens, with 360,000 teenagers and children in the US taking up the habit per year. But would the vaccine be given to all children or only a selected few? 'There are civil liberties issues,' says Amanda Sandford of Action on Smoking and Health (ASH), an anti-smoking charity. 'How will we decide which children are most at risk of becoming smokers?' Instead she favours education as a way of discouraging children from smoking. Mark Soufliers of Florida-based Nabi Biopharmaceuticals is also cautious. 'It is very difficult to know what is the right age to give the vaccine to children, and whether you'd need to give regular boosters. Also, how much right does a child have to say no to vaccination?'

There are also worries about giving the vaccine to long-term adult smokers. Since the vaccine doesn't get rid of the cravings for cigarettes, will dependent smokers simply try to beat the vaccine's antibodies by smoking more? Gary Norwith, Nabi's clinical director, says this would be virtually impossible. 'You'd have to stick an entire pack of cigarettes in your mouth and smoke for hours to override the antibodies,' he says.

How the vaccine works

- ....

- ....

Arguments for giving it to children

- ....

- ....

Arguments against giving it to children

- ....

- ....

- ....

- ....

LINKED SUMMARY

Using the ideas in your notes, write a paragraph of no more than 70 words outlining the pros and cons of giving the smoking vaccine to children. Use your own words as far as possible.

Developing a mature approach to study

EXAMINER'S TIP

Students sometimes become very competitive with each other, comparing marks and feeling annoyed if a classmate does better than they do in a test. A little competition in the class can indeed give extra motivation and spur you on to try harder.

However, another way you can improve your skills is to be cooperative with each other, rather than directly competitive. Talking with a friend about the process of learning helps you reflect on what you are learning, and develops a more mature attitude to study. Discussing things in this way helps you think through the topics you are studying, which deepens and strengthens your understanding. This is particularly important in English, when there may not be simple 'right' or 'wrong' answers.

Reflecting on your learning also helps you become more objective about your progress. You will think more clearly about how your skills are improving and the ways in which you want to develop them further.

Read the article about zoo cats. Write a summary outlining the signs of stress which big cats in zoos may show and what could be done to make them feel more comfortable in a zoo environment. Write about 100 words and use your own words as far as possible.

Why zoo cats lose their cool

Lions and tigers are stars of the show at most zoos. But the stress of celebrity status can cause them and other big cats on display to behave abnormally.

Researchers in the US have found that cats living near visitor areas are more likely to be disturbed in their behaviour. For example, during the day they may pace aimlessly back and forth. They also spend an unusual amount of time cleaning themselves, licking themselves and generally grooming. They are also noticeably more vigilant, pricking up their ears and moving around as though they feel the need to be on guard against threat. This is all strange and abnormal behaviour for naturally nocturnal felines which should not be at all suspicious during this part of the day. In fact, big cats are usually asleep, resting or dozing during the day and active and watchful at night.

The findings highlight the dilemma that zoos face when the welfare and happiness of the animals they look after are at odds with the paying public's desire to get a close-up view of a lioness yawning or her cubs suckling. It seems as though disturbed behaviour in animals may well continue unless positive action is taken to improve the environment in which zoos house big cats and their smaller cousins in the cat family, such as caracals and bobcats. While a lot of work has gone into designing accommodation for primates and studying how visitors affect the health and well-being of monkeys, gorillas or chimpanzees, cats have been largely ignored.

Jennifer Ryback of James Madison University in Harrisonburg, Virginia, studied seven species of cat kept at the National Zoological Park in Washington, DC. All the cats, including lions, tigers, caracals and fishing cats, showed abnormal behaviour, and Ryback found that those housed near the public spend more time acting unnaturally than those that live further away.

'Typically a cat will be resting during the day, which is certainly not what the public wants to see,' says Ryback. When the cats seem distant or aloof and appear to be ignoring people, visitors actively try to attract their attention by waving or calling to them. They hope to get a reaction from the cats, such as hearing them roar or spring up a nearby tree. But the gesturing and shouting from observers make the animals even more stressed and irritated, putting them on the alert and making them pace around and groom more.

As well as improving the cats' enclosures by redesigning the space, including better use of ponds, bushes and trees, Ryback thinks zoos could greatly enhance the quality of life for their cats by displaying notices explaining how to behave near the animals. In other words, people should show no excitement, not try to attract the animals or make a noise near them. Zoo attendants or keepers should also watch out in particular for visitors behaving inappropriately near the animals and intervene at once. Ryback also suspects that keeping visitors just a little further away from the animals could make a big difference to the cats with virtually no effect on people's enjoyment.

....

....

....

....

....

....

....

....

....

....

....

....

....

....

Punctuation

EXAMINER'S TIP

Correct punctuation makes a difference to the clarity of your work. In the exam it is expected that basic punctuation such as full stops and capital letters will be accurate. A full stop is used to show the end of a complete sentence. Try to get into the habit of putting in the full stops as you go along, by 'hearing' what you are writing in your head. Don't leave it until the end of your writing and then put them in – you are much more likely to put the full stops in the wrong place if you do this.

Remember to use capital letters for the following: the first letter in a sentence, people's names and titles, nationalities, names of places, days of the week, names of months, book and film titles, and the pronoun I.

Try noticing how the punctuation is used when you read English books and newspapers. This is an easy way to reinforce your understanding of how punctuation makes meaning clear.

You are going to give a talk to a group of school friends hoping to take part in a whale-watching activity holiday, observing whales, porpoises and dolphins. Using information from the article, write a set of notes under the headings given, as a basis for your talk.

The thrill of watching whales

When I volunteered to spend a summer on a land-based whale-watching project in the West of Scotland, the project secretary warned me, 'You have to be able to detect the whales from the shore – it's not as easy as you think.' Although I assumed I was well-qualified for the job, at the start of the project I often imagined I could see dorsal fins in the dark tip of every wave and dolphins leaping in the wake created by every passing boat. I had a few embarrassing moments screaming 'Whale!' before realising that what I was pointing out were only waves breaking over submerged rocks, not sea creatures at all!

After a while, I trained my eyes to 'see' – to distinguish between waves splashing over rocks and the rolling movement of whales underwater. I spent a lot of time just watching the sea through my binoculars, looking actively for anything that indicated sea life below. Learning more about the marine environment increased my ability to differentiate, especially in regard to the tides and currents, as these draw whales to certain areas. My binoculars enabled me to spot the fins of a porpoise against the darkness of the sea, and without a good pair of binoculars I definitely would have missed out on lots of stunning marine life.

In addition, I eventually realised that the birds provide us with signals that cetaceans – whales, dolphins and porpoises – may be in the area. Where there is a flock of feeding seabirds such as seagulls or gannets, there is often a whale feeding beneath them. Gannets are really easy to spot from a distance – they drop out of the sky at speeds of up to 100 kph, spearing the surface and sending bursts of water up behind them. I also learned how to take my time, to be patient, peaceful and quiet so that the whales are oblivious to and undisturbed by my presence. One of my favourite moments occurred when I was sitting quietly by the sea on the Isle of Mull and a group of porpoises came in so close to the shoreline I could hear the gentle puffs of their breath.

If you want to try this activity, it is worth organising and planning carefully for whale-watching. I recommend having a notebook and pencil nearby to record details of what you've seen and the environmental conditions at the time. This is not only a helpful aid in general, but you can also contribute your sightings to research projects such as the Sea Watch Foundation, that are monitoring the distribution of whales and dolphins.

Despite the early disappointments I had, I think there is undoubtedly something very special about watching whales. Nothing can compare with the secret thrill and the tranquillity of seeing a wild animal just doing its own thing.

How to get the most out of watching whales, porpoises and dolphins

- ....
- ....
- ....
- ....
- ....
- ....

Useful equipment for this activity

- ....
- ....

LINKED SUMMARY

Using the ideas in your notes, write a paragraph of no more than 70 words explaining how whale watching can be made as satisfying as possible. Use your own words as far as possible.

Selecting relevant information

As no word limit is given in the instructions for the note-taking exercise, students sometimes copy out long extracts from the text, hoping in this way to 'cover' the required information for the answer. This strategy does not produce good notes because the examiner wants to see that you have the skill of extracting only the relevant information. Be selective. If you copy out a large amount from the text, you will not get the best marks, even if what you copy contains some of the relevant points.

Your notes should be clear and concise, and you do not need to write complete sentences. You should find one piece of information for each bullet point on the exam paper (usually eight).

Don't worry if you can't find information to answer the question in the first part of the text. The question may be designed to require information that comes later in the text.

Read the article about the Sabi-Sand game reserve and write a summary outlining the positive steps that are being taken to ensure the wildlife habitat is suitably protected and developed. Write about 100 words and use your own words as far as possible.

Bisected by the Sabi and Sand rivers, the Sabi-Sand game reserve in South Africa is one of the richest wildlife regions in the African continent. Over 200 species of mammals and 350 different birds can be found in its vast plains, grasslands and forest.

The Sabi-Sand game reserve

I spoke to Michael Rattray, chairman of the Sabi-Sand management committee, about the management policies for such a diverse habitat. 'If in a thousand years' time the reserve is still a wonderful habitat for wildlife, then we will have succeeded in our mission. We have a programme of ongoing management and various measures are being put in place. These include tackling the problem of erosion. In 1996 we had abnormally high rainfall – 1300 ml instead of the expected 500 ml. This could have been absolutely devastating. However we have successfully combated erosion using gabion stretchers, which are cylindrical wire baskets filled with rocks. These have proved a simple and effective method of improving drainage. We have also used a lot of old aerial photographs, which have helped us return the land to its earlier state. This meant recreating open grassland areas to attract herds of wildebeest, zebra, buffalo, antelope and their predators.'

In addition to these measures, the reserve employs a wide range of local workers in a variety of occupations. Building staff accommodation of any sort, even small bungalows, would have made a big impact on the environment and would have gone against the objective of keeping the reserve as natural as possible. Instead, transport is provided so employees can live a normal, free and unrestricted life with their families outside the area, and human impact is kept to a minimum.

Visitors to the reserve spend about six hours a day in open 4x4 vehicles, observing wildlife on game drives. They are accompanied by a ranger and a local tracker. Part of the management policy is to employ only rangers and trackers of the highest standard. The ranger is highly educated, often with a degree in botany, biology, bushcraft, zoology and even astronomy. Tourists can listen to 'ranger-speak' on the two-way radio as, with ear-piece tucked into his ear, the ranger communicates with fellow-rangers. Animals are referred to by their Shangaan names: *ingwe* (leopard), *shumba* (lion) and *khankankha* (cheetah). The local Shangaan trackers are chosen for their keen eyesight and in-depth knowledge of the bush. Ranger and tracker together make a professional team. I shall never forget the moment on a game drive when a cheetah with her five cubs was pointed out to me. She was lying in a sea of long yellow grass, her markings almost invisible. We got close enough to hear her purr.

The Sabi-Sand reserve offers the visitor a taste of Africa as it used to be before mankind's incursions, a place where animals co-exist in accordance with natural cycles, with no fear of humans. It is impossible to quantify the therapeutic benefits of spending time – however briefly – in such an environment.

....

....

....

....

....

....

....

....

....

....

....

....

....

....

Specialised and technical terms

EXAMINER'S TIP

Sometimes a text will contain a specialised or technical term, such as *gabion stretchers*, which a student could not be expected to know. If this is the case, the specialised term is explained within the text, as it is here (*cylindrical wire baskets filled with rocks*).

When you write a summary, you may need to include either the specialised term or the explanation of it. Do not use both – you should choose either one way or the other of referring to it. The specialised term itself is usually briefer than the definition, so using it in your summary will help you to write more concisely.

Read the article about dog training and complete the notes under the headings given.

Dogs on the defensive

An expert offers advice

A lady contacted me the other day and said, 'I've recently bought a young puppy. When I take her out for a walk around my neighbourhood, she turns hostile and aggressive if children try to approach. I don't know what to do about it. Can you help?'

The majority of 'aggressive' dogs are just being defensive, because they feel scared, trapped or threatened in some way. The dog is probably feeling frightened by the children and is using canine language to 'tell' them to go away. Unfortunately, children do not understand what the dog is 'saying'. The animal resorts to growling and biting in an attempt to drive them away.

The fact is that a young dog learns quickly that aggressive behaviour works – it makes the threat disappear. So a dog will keep on being aggressive when he feels threatened, unless you do something about it. You have to act to stop him becoming aggressive before it becomes a learned routine.

The first rule of dog ownership is to handle your pet all over every day. If a dog cannot be touched in this way without becoming alarmed, it is a very serious problem. At some point he is going to need treatment from a vet and a physical examination will be impossible. Also, one day a stranger will approach the dog and try to pat him, with disastrous consequences. So, handle your pet daily. You should stroke the dog's fur all over, lift his tail, paws and so on.

I also see pets who are aggressive behaving disrespectfully in the family home. They have free access to rooms, jump on furniture and steal food. Dogs need to learn that their owners are in charge and to obey their commands. Dogs can be taught to be more obedient through positive reinforcement. Praise and pat your dog when he obeys a command, or give him a little treat like a tasty biscuit. Treating dogs in this way can have a dramatic effect and make them much better companions.

The best solution for dogs who are nervous and agitated around other dogs is to find a training school where the instructor has experience of dealing with the problem. At a training school, your dog will be introduced to other dogs in a controlled way so that he no longer experiences them as a threat. Games and gentle play will deter him from acting defensively. It is a good idea, too, for the dog trainer to accompany you and your pet on one of your daily walks in your locality, to observe you both and give advice. It can take a lot of commitment, time and money to rehabilitate a dog that is difficult to control, but it is well worth doing.

Why dogs may be aggressive

• ....

• ....

How to have a well-behaved dog

• ....

• ....

• ....

What dog training schools and trainers can offer

• ....

• ....

• ....

LINKED SUMMARY

Using the ideas in your notes, write a paragraph of no more than 70 words explaining how aggressive dog behaviour can be improved. Use your own words as far as possible.

Predicting the content of a text

EXAMINER'S TIP

Look carefully at any headings, sub-headings, pictures or charts to get a general idea of what the text is about before you start to read.

Think carefully about the purpose of the text and the writer's intended audience. Is it designed to give the reader help and advice, or information and explanation?

When you have recognised who the writer is writing for and why, you will be more able to predict the possible content. You will also be more receptive and alert to the type of vocabulary used, and this will help you understand the text better. For example, in this text about dog training you can expect to find lots of vocabulary specifically relating to dogs and their behaviour in a domestic setting. (Examples here include *puppy*, *aggressive*, *canine*, *growling*, *biting*, *stroke*, *fur*, *command*, *obedient*, *praise*, *pat*.)

Read the article about rose-growing. Then write a summary outlining how roses were used in previous civilisations and why the rose is called the 'flower of life'. You should write about 100 words and use your own words as far as possible.

The rose
Queen of all flowers

The ancient Egyptians appear to be among the first early civilisations to learn how to grow roses. In 1888, at Hawara in the El Faiyum region of Egypt, two-thousand-year-old roses were found in ancient graves. The discovery suggested roses were an important part of the elaborate burial ceremony which took place when an important person died. The roses found in the tombs are thought by modern experts to be the oldest preserved flowers ever found in the entire world. They must have been cut and dried before opening so that they would remain undamaged. Over the centuries, the roses had shrunk and wrinkled into tight balls, but on careful examination it was discovered that the petals themselves were hardly damaged – not a grain of pollen had been lost.

Egypt's expertise in mass-cultivation of roses in early times led to the flowers becoming an important export product. At the height of the Roman Empire, Egypt exported enormous quantities of the blooms to the Roman courts. Wealthy Romans loved to indulge in the beautiful colours, soft texture and sensuous fragrances of roses and they would strew the floors of their main halls with layers of rose petals.

The Romans eventually attempted to cultivate their own roses and, after much trial and error, they mastered the art of mass cultivation. Egypt then decided to concentrate on growing grain instead of roses. Economic conditions meant that grain soon took over as the number-one agricultural product of the Nile valley.

Roses were appreciated in other early civilisations too, including Greece and Persia. They are a decorative feature on coins, sculpture, vases and ornaments dating back thousands of years. There is also evidence that roses were highly valued in China. The Chinese believed that fluids extracted from roses could be used to help treat a wide range of illnesses, from toothache and earache to skin and chest diseases. The healing properties of the flowers were recorded in extensive detail in their manuscripts.

In the modern world, the rose has not lost its popularity as the 'Queen of Flowers' – the name given to it by the Greek poetess Sappho. A rose is a very romantic gift, and to this day more roses are sold than any other flower. Modern techniques have enabled botanists to create ever more beautiful hybrids, combining selected features of parent plants. Transportation by air makes it possible to grow roses in countries with favourable climates and sell them within 24 hours in lucrative markets all over the world. Tons of roses are transported this way every week. Roses from Ecuador can be bought in Holland, even though that country itself has an enormous rose-growing business.

The rose has everything a plant can have: roots, stem, leaves, petals, thorns, colour and scent. The combination of beautiful flowers and sharp, prickly thorns is seen by some as symbolising the opposites of beauty and ugliness, happiness and pain, love and hatred. This rich symbolism surely makes the rose deserving of its other name: the flower of life.

....

....

....

....

....

....

....

....

....

....

....

....

....

....

....

....

Identifying key words

EXAMINER'S TIP

Students are usually advised to underline the key words in the question but are sometimes unclear what a key word is. Key words carry important information. They include verbs such as *describe*, *explain*, *outline*, *compare* and *contrast* – verbs indicating the kind of analysis of the text that you have to do.

The key verb is followed by other content words which carry meaning. In between the key words are less important grammar words such as prepositions and articles.

In the question on the opposite page, the words *in previous civilisations* are crucial because they tell you that your summary should not include information about the use of roses today. Similarly, the words *how roses were used* show that you should not include the information about the growing of grain in the Nile valley (not about roses), or the fact that the roses found in 1888 in the ancient graves were in good condition (not about their use).

Read the article about the tea tree and complete the notes under the headings provided.

A Natural Antiseptic

Charlotte Baxter investigates the new cure-all of our times.

In pharmacies and health food shops all over the world you will see products containing tea tree oil. It is a wonderful antiseptic, good for acne, dry itchy skin, bruises and burns. As an antibacterial agent, it will aid the treatment of dermatitis and fungal infections.

I had no idea where the oil came from and in my innocence imagined a fruit similar to an olive from which an oil would be extracted. So when I was invited to visit Birditt Farm, a tea tree plantation near the small town of Dimbulah, 7114 km west of Cairns in Queensland, Australia, I was intrigued and interested.

The tea tree is a low, conifer-like bush with a papery bark, and its flowers consist of cream-coloured spikes. The oil is distilled from the needles.

The plants are grown from very tiny seeds, which take from five to seven days to germinate. At about an inch high, the tiny seedlings are transplanted into trays for the next stage of the growing process. The seedlings are kept first in an intensive greenhouse atmosphere and then moved to cooler shade houses, rather like large open tents.

The permanent staff at Birditt farm are a jolly bunch and more than willing to let visitors help with looking after the seedlings. I was involved with transplanting the tiny seedlings into larger containers. This method, known as pricking-out, needs a fair amount of dexterity, and I am afraid I damaged the first few plants I handled. However, I soon learned to handle them appropriately, using the minimum of pressure, and enjoyed chatting to the other workers about their families and lives in the area.

Tea tree oil production is extremely labour-intensive, since pricking-out and care during the growing stage, including weeding, have to be done by hand. At busy times casual labour – usually backpackers or students looking for temporary work during college vacations – is employed. They are very enthusiastic at first, but soon tire in the hot, often humid, atmosphere of the glasshouses and have to pace themselves to get through the work required.

Irrigation is by large, specialised machines: giant 'walking' irrigators. This watering process has to be monitored from time to time to ensure that the plants are receiving the right amount of water.

When the tea trees are strong bushy plants, four to six feet tall, they are cut down to within a foot of the ground and put into large bins ready for the steam distillation process.

The steam raises the temperature of the oil in the leaves, and the oil then evaporates into a water-cooled condenser. After the vapour has condensed, the resulting oil and water mixture is discharged into an oil separator. Here the oil floats on the water and is finally drawn off.

The precious fluid is then put into sterile stainless steel or plastic-lined drums. The oil is stored in these drums after the process of extraction is complete before being shipped to a distribution centre.

The use of tea tree oil is fast increasing globally – its healing properties are Australia's gift to the making of a healthier world.

Properties of tea tree oil

• ....

• ....

How the distillation process works

• ....

• ....

• ....

• ....

• ....

• ....

LINKED SUMMARY

Using the ideas in your notes, write a paragraph of no more than 70 words describing the tea tree and outlining the properties of its oil. Use your own words as far as possible.

Describing a process

EXAMINER'S TIP

When describing a process, take care that you have understood and covered each stage of the process. In the note-taking question, there will be one bullet point for each stage. Look out for words like *First*, *then*, *next*, *after* and *finally*, as these can be helpful clues to the sequence of events in the process.

Passive forms are common in descriptions of processes, and you may find them useful in your notes. Examples in the article are: *the oil and water mixture is discharged* and *the oil is drawn off*.

Finally, read through your notes to make sure the points make sense and that they are in the correct order. Also check that they do not repeat each other.

Read the article about mangoes. Then write a summary describing how various parts of the mango tree are used, and outlining how the problems in producing mangoes for the world's supermarkets can be solved. Write about 100 words. Try to use your own words as far as possible.

The mangoes in your trolley

Wild mangoes come from the foothills of the Himalayas. They are by far the most important fruit in India, and have been cultivated there for 4000 years. The arrival of the mango tree in other parts of the world was probably due to the Portuguese who carried mangoes via Goa to Africa, from where they eventually reached the New World. Mango trees are now so well established in many tropical countries that it might appear that they have always been there.

Like many tropical trees, the mango tree is a multi-purpose commodity. Its timber is used in boat building, and its leaves can be fed to cattle in moderation.

Most of the mango crop is consumed in the areas where it is grown, but in recent years mangoes have gained in popularity across the world as people in temperate climates become increasingly eager to savour the delights of the fresh fruit.

The global market for mangoes is potentially very lucrative, and mango producers are keen to exploit the fruit's growing popularity. Modern shoppers appreciate the fruit's high nutritional value (the mango is a good source of vitamins A and C, protein, fructose and fibre), but also expect it to look and taste perfect. Unfortunately for producers, the seedlings of mangoes are extremely variable in quality, and many have to be rejected as below the standard required for propagation. For mass-cultivation, producers now select only the best quality seedlings which have the most chance of developing into good quality fruit.

Although the mango tree has spread from its native Himalayan foothills to all of the tropics, delivering the fresh fruit to the world's supermarkets presents a

challenge, as it does not travel well. Producers transport the fruit by speedy but costly air freight for minimum delay rather than risk the cheaper but slower road or shipping routes which, although saving money, can result in damage to the fruit.

Mangoes are usually in storage for some time after their arrival at their destination. The fruit must be kept cold or the sweet, juicy flesh will soon become over-ripe and the mangoes will be unfit for sale. Fortunately, extremely effective refrigeration is now available and this is the best way of preventing the fruit from deteriorating before it reaches the supermarket shelves.

Many of the mangoes in our supermarkets come from plantations established in Kenya. These mangoes are sold in the shops at quite a high price relative to other fruit, but the cost reflects the expense of air transport and top quality refrigeration. Fortunately for the producer, shoppers are prepared to pay extra to enjoy this most delicious of tropical fruit at its best.

....

....

....

....

....

....

....

....

....

....

....

....

....

....

Using your own words

Remember that, although the instructions in the exam tell you to 'use your own words as far as possible', words of technical meaning such as *seedlings* and *propagation* can be taken directly from the text. Moreover, the examiner will not expect you to find substitutes for every word in the text, provided you can show you have sufficient range of vocabulary to use your own words quite often.

In assessing how good your writing is, the examiner will also look in general at your overall control of language, and the way you have reorganised and structured sentences.

Read the article about the history of chocolate and complete the notes under the headings provided.

Sweet Talk

The botanical name of the cocoa tree, from which chocolate is made, is *Theobroma cacao*. The first word is Greek for 'food of the gods'. Depending on whom you believe, this seductive substance is an effective mood lifter and good for the heart, or the cause of spots, migraine, obesity and stressed-out nerves. But almost everyone believes it is one of the most irresistible foodstuffs ever produced.

Now, we learn that chocolate has been around for a lot longer than was previously thought. Traces of it have been found in pots discovered in Mayan graves in Mexico, some of which date back to 600BC, which pushes back the earliest chemical evidence of chocolate by more than 1000 years.

Chocolate is made from the seeds or 'beans' of the cocoa tree – the leathery cocoa pod contains up to 100 beans. Aztecs in Mexico and Mayans in Belize worshipped the tree and used its beans as a form of currency. They also hit upon the idea of crushing the beans, boiling them in water, then adding spices and drinking the resulting hot, frothy liquid. In the 16th century, Spaniards who landed in Mexico wrote of how the Aztec emperor Moctezuma drank chocolate 'from pure gold cups ... with great reverence'.

In 1519 the explorer Hernan Cortes sent three chests full of cocoa beans to the Emperor Charles V, complete with instructions on how to use them. Later, Sir Francis Drake brought a ton of cocoa beans back to England. They were destined for the court of Queen Elizabeth I, but were mistaken for sheep droppings and thrown into Plymouth harbour.

Gradually, chocolate became a part of European life. Rich aristocrats and the privileged elite adopted the habit of drinking it during the day. It was not until sugar was added to the brew, however, and it was served in the coffee houses that chocolate was bought and enjoyed by the general public. Cocoa plantations sprang up all over the world to meet the growing demand and, as the export of cocoa beans increased, chocolate became more easily available to ordinary people in Europe.

The conversion of chocolate from a drink to a food began in the 1700s when cocoa was added to cakes and ice-cream. The first attempts at making solid chocolate came in the early 1800s when cocoa beans were ground into a powder, heated, sweetened and pressed into a mould. The resulting product resembled the chocolate truffles we eat today, but had a short shelf life.

It was a Dutch chemist and food scientist, Coenrad Van Houten, who in 1825 perfected the extraction of cocoa butter from beans, which enabled the production of solid bars we would recognise as chocolate today. In the 1880s, Rudolph Lindt of Switzerland started adding extra cocoa to make a product that melted at 36°C. This is just a degree below the core temperature of the human body, so for the first time chocolate would melt in the mouth but not in the pocket on a warm day. Around the same time Daniel Peter, a Swiss candy-maker, added condensed milk developed by Henri Nestlé to chocolate, making a sweeter and smoother variety of what is now one of the world's favourite foods.

Chocolate is produced from:

• ....

Why the chocolate drink increased in popularity in Europe

• ....

• ....

• ....

Problem with the first solid chocolate ever made

• ....

19th-century developments in the production of better solid chocolate

• ....

• ....

• ....

LINKED SUMMARY

Using the ideas in your notes, write a paragraph of no more than 70 words explaining why ordinary people began to enjoy chocolate drinks, and describing the experiments which took place in the nineteenth century to improve solid chocolate. Use your own words as far as possible.

Puns and idioms in titles

You probably remember being told to look carefully at the heading or title of a text before beginning to read. This is good advice because the title usually contains important information. However, titles sometimes can be difficult to understand fully. This may be because of techniques the writer uses, especially devices which aim at a humorous effect, such as puns – using words or phrases with more than one meaning.

The author of this article chooses the title 'Sweet Talk' because it has two meanings. It can convey the idea that the article is about sweets or chocolate, but it is also an idiom meaning the affectionate language we use with close friends to flatter them and to get what we want.

When you next find a heading surprising or strange, consider whether there could be an idiomatic aspect involved. You can become more familiar with puns and idioms through listening to popular songs in English, watching films and reading widely.

Read the article about students who spend a year abroad at a foreign university as part of their course. Write a summary explaining what projects students are expected to produce from this year, the practical ways the home university prepares them for leaving, and how they maintain links with their tutors at home. You should write about 100 words and use your own words as far as possible.

Young ambassadors

Contrary to the beliefs of many of its opponents, going abroad to study at an overseas university whilst on an undergraduate degree programme is definitely not an opportunity for a lazy year off. The year abroad provides students with a remarkable period of linguistic and cultural immersion in the host community. It allows them to gain first-hand insights into the history, culture and society of the host country, as well as an opportunity to improve their academic skills. Besides attending lectures and doing coursework while abroad, students are required to complete a cultural and linguistic assignment for their home university.

The year overseas is also important to students on a personal level. It calls upon untapped reserves of tenacity, fortitude, perseverance and initiative, and requires a spirit of open-mindedness, curiosity and willingness to fit into a new life. The diversity of the experiences certainly broadens the minds of most undergraduates. Many language students now spend their year abroad in Spanish-speaking Latin America, French territories in the Caribbean or the Indian Ocean, or the Russian-speaking states that once formed part of the Soviet Union.

Home universities spend a great deal of time making sure their students have a realistic idea of what the year abroad will be like – they certainly do not simply wave goodbye to them for a year.

It is important, for example, that students do not expect the foreign institution to mirror their home university or indeed be like it in any way. In many universities, students are provided with a series of briefings throughout their second year of study, which include checklists, guides, handbooks and web-based information. Students who went abroad the previous year and have now returned answer questions on their experiences.

Although university staff make great efforts to reduce the culture shock some students feel on arrival in another country, the students have responsibilities and obligations too. When overseas, they have a duty to keep in close touch with their home departments, through answering regular questionnaires, for example.

Maintaining contact with their personal tutor at home via email, telephone or letter is essential. Tutors can only act quickly in giving support if they are kept informed by their students about their situation.

In my experience as a lecturer, returning students are usually brimming with exciting tales to tell of their experiences abroad. They return much more competent, with a more mature and considered approach, and have acquired some valuable life skills.

....

....

....

....

....

....

....

....

....

....

....

....

....

....

Summarising more difficult texts

Sometimes students say they find some texts harder than others. Perhaps this is because the information is more involved, the language level seems a bit higher, or the topic is unfamiliar.

If you find a text hard, don't panic. The most important thing is to make sure you have understood the question set, and then try to get a good general idea of the contents. Also, try to be methodical in your approach, take the material step by step and make sure that, in your answer, you have covered all aspects of the question.

Even the more difficult-looking texts can be done very well when students follow the simple rules of not rushing, being careful about detail, and making really sure that they have not missed out anything which is important for the answer. At the other extreme, students can lose marks because they rush through a text thinking it is 'easy', only to make silly mistakes because they do not take enough care and forget to follow the simple rules.

Read the article about a teenage girl who survived for three days in the Australian rainforest. Then make **two** short notes under each of the headings given.

LOST ON THE MOUNTAIN

19-YEAR-OLD TRAINEE BEAUTICIAN TELLS HOW SHE SURVIVED FOR THREE DAYS IN DENSE RAINFOREST

After three days of searching for Louise Saunders on the slopes of Mount Tyson in tropical northern Queensland, most people's greatest hope was to find her lying injured somewhere among the mountain's rocky gullies. The last thing they were expecting was for her to walk out of the rainforest at a local rubbish dump. She was scratched, cut, bruised and hungry but otherwise unharmed after her ordeal.

'It was an experience and an adventure, but I would never want to go through it again,' said Louise, from Kidderminster, England, who was spending time fruit-picking and travelling in Australia.

Part of her remarkable escape was due to the weather conditions. It was unusually warm and dry. Also, the many streams running down the sides of the 2,165 foot Mount Tyson allowed her to refill the two water bottles she had brought with her. 'I didn't really sleep,' said Louise. 'It was just so cold at night.'

Louise appears to have crossed over the long north-south ridge of the mountain before following a gorge down the southern slopes, to the tea-tree swamps surrounding the Cardwell Shire tip.

The greatest mystery was how anyone could be so hard to find on a mountain almost surrounded by roads and covering only a few square miles. Police say the thick vegetation near the streams may have hidden her from search parties and helicopters. More baffling is the failure to spot her when she deliberately stayed out in the open. 'I stayed in the same place the whole day,' she said. 'I chose to climb to the top of a waterfall because it was really open. I thought if they were going to see me, they would notice me there.'

The workers who found her at Cardwell Shire dump said they were dumbfounded at her survival in the harsh rainforest. 'She was just yelling out when she saw us,' said Louis Maund, who was on duty when she appeared outside the fence surrounding the dump.

Louise's mother told TV reporters, 'Louise was so resourceful. I am so proud of her. She remained calm when a grown man would have been terrified.' This area of Queensland is known for its unforgiving wildlife and the treacherous plants. The jungle is infested with taipan, one of the most poisonous snakes in the world. Less dangerous but irritating all the same is the wait-a-while vine. The vine's tendrils carry sharp hooks which lacerate bare skin.

The search parties moved through the forest in groups of four, armed with walkie-talkies and keeping close together in case of danger. 'You're clambering over these big boulders with loose rocks underfoot,' said searcher Kieran Falnaga, 23, who admitted he was exhausted after a few hours of searching. George Guido, 28, another member of the search party, said, 'We were hacking through the undergrowth – we couldn't see more than two feet in front of us.'

Louise had been fruit-picking on local farms to finance her extended trip, and had already visited Perth, Darwin, Uluru and Alice Springs.

What helped Louise to survive

- ....

- ....

How Louise tried to attract attention

- ....

- ....

The special dangers to walkers exploring the area

- ....

- ....

How the search for Louise was organised

- ....

- ....

LINKED SUMMARY

Using the ideas in your notes, write a paragraph of no more than 70 words outlining what helped Louise to survive on the mountain, and how she tried to attract the attention of people searching for her. Use your own words as far as possible.

Dealing with unknown words

EXAMINER'S TIP

Don't worry if you don't understand every word in a text. You can understand a text well without knowing every single word.

In this text, perhaps you found the words *gullies* and *gorge* unfamiliar, for example. If you come across strange words such as these, try to make a guess at their meaning by studying the context. Here the word *gullies* is associated with places on the mountain where Louise might have fallen, so the situation being described might give you a good enough idea of what *gullies* might be.

Also, even if there is some unusual or rare vocabulary in the text, exam questions usually avoid targeting it for the answer. The required answers are based on straightforward language which, as an IGCSE student, you could reasonably be expected to know. Difficult language from the text is avoided.

Read the article about a girl who lost her feet in babyhood. Write a summary of about 100 words outlining how she has coped with the effects of her disability, the differences between her 'old' and 'new' artificial legs, and the effect of her new legs on her life. Use your own words as far as possible.

My daughter can achieve whatever she wants

Vanessa Hill lost her feet from illness at such a young age that she never knew what it was like to have them. At 13 months old she was fitted with a set of prosthetic (artificial) limbs to assist her in learning to take her first baby steps. 'I should have been pleased, but the artificial legs were horrible,' says Vanessa's mother, Jan. 'They weren't even the same colour as her skin and were cold to the touch.'

Problems began when Vanessa was older. 'I'd see people walking past me and they would stare and make comments. It upset me, and hurt Mum too, to see me so upset,' says Vanessa. 'Mum told me to ignore what unkind people said and, in time, I was able to do that. When activities at school came up, like swimming and skiing, I was reluctant to take part but my mother encouraged me so much I decided to give the sports a go anyway, and now I enjoy them.'

'She was so brave and determined', says Jan. 'At first she took the teasing to heart and was very upset, but she just wouldn't give up. At home we gave her all the support we could and I think that made a big difference.'

A couple of years ago, the family saw a television programme about a girl in Cape Town, Laura Giddings, who had lost her leg in an explosion at a restaurant. Jan explains: 'Laura had been fitted with a silicone leg which was much more realistic-looking than the prosthetic limbs Vanessa had. I cried as I thought what a massive difference such natural-type legs could have on Vanessa's life. But with two other children to look after as well as Vanessa, there was no way we

could afford to pay for silicone legs. We would have had to spend £5,500 on new legs for her every six months, as she is still growing.'

Not long afterwards, the school support worker rang the family and asked if there was anything she could do to help. 'I found myself spilling out everything about the private treatment', says Jan. A few weeks later the support worker called again to say she had come up with a plan to organise some fund-raising events to get Vanessa new legs. 'I was completely overwhelmed. The school organised raffles, cake sales and sponsored events. People we had never met sent donations. Every day we got cards from well-wishers, and the cheques just kept arriving.'

'When enough money had been raised, I contacted the orthopaedic centre and Vanessa was measured for her new legs. When the consultant showed us the sort of silicone legs Vanessa could have, we couldn't believe how realistic they looked. The specialists could match her exact skin tone.'

'I've got loads more confidence and love going shopping for shoes and clothes,' says Vanessa. 'My legs look so real, and if you touch them they feel warm, like proper legs. But the best part is finally being able to do anything without having to worry about how my legs look. Now I'm just like everyone else.'

....

....

....

....

....

....

....

....

....

....

....

....

....

....

....

Using appropriate tenses and correct names

EXAMINER'S TIP

Tenses are important in showing the time aspect of a story. In this story, for example, past tenses are used to show what happened before Vanessa got her new legs, whereas the present tense is used to describe her situation and feelings since she had new legs fitted.

When you write your summary, be careful to use the appropriate tenses to talk about the past and the present. Study the words in the question carefully – these will give you ideas about the right tenses to use too.

You should also be careful when several different people are referred to by name in a text. If you have to write about these people, be careful to use their correct names and try not to mix them up. If you do this, your writing will be clear and easy to understand.

Your head teacher has asked you to give a talk to a group of school leavers at a careers information evening. The topic of the talk is 'Taking a gap year'. (A 'gap year' is a year between leaving school and going to college or university.) Using information from the article, write a set of notes under the headings given, as a basis for your talk.

Taking a Gap Year

After exams, going to university or getting your first job isn't the only adventure to go for. Robert Bates said 'yes' to a year out in another country. Here he talks about his experiences.

I was pleased with my exam results which secured me a place at university to study engineering. But I also wanted to travel before starting my course. I thought carefully about the kind of trip to do – just backpacking around the globe didn't appeal. Then a friend of mine told me about organisations which help students take a gap year.

Raleigh International, for instance, has projects all over the world for 18–25-year-olds. You can do so many different things, from deer-trekking in Uganda to rice-picking in China. I also heard about the Schools Exploring Society. It has three foreign expeditions a year, taking 16–20-year-olds on science and nature trips. I love being outdoors, and a mountaineering expedition to Alaska was on offer. I decided this was my chance to see the world and I signed up immediately.

There was one problem, though. To be allowed on the trip, I had to raise a large amount of money for my fare and expenses. It was daunting, but I thought about how to meet the target. To help me focus on getting temporary paid work, I listed my skills and personal qualities. In the end, I washed cars, worked in a café and also sold off some of my old books, clothes and CDs. Actually, I only made the target six days before departure. Then, just before I was due to go, I started worrying. Can I do this? Am I fit enough? What if I see a bear?!

Seventy of us travelled to Alaska. The first two days after arrival were spent in a school hall preparing our equipment and five tonnes of food. Then, in groups of 12, we headed for the Talkeetna mountains. They were stunning. On the trip we dug paths, identified plant species and analysed soil acidity. It was tiring, but I kept thinking 'I can't believe I'm here.' Then we trekked over a glacier 6000 feet high. It was hard work and very cold, but incredible too.

After 13 years in the same school with the same friends, it was nerve-wracking but inspiring to be thousands of miles away, talking to people with different ideas on life. I learned a lot about tolerance – accepting other people for what they are. We had to help each other and it made me less selfish, as I had to consider other people before myself.

Looking back, a gap year was so right for me. I'm sure I would have burnt out in my first year of university if I'd gone straight from school with no break from studying. Instead of being distracted from my studies, my gap year has made me more able to concentrate and better at analysing information. Now, whenever I'm worried about anything, I think 'I did Alaska – I can do this!'

Organisations that offer gap year projects

• ....

• ....

Before trying to get work, it is useful to

• ....

• ....

How a gap year can develop your character

• ....

• ....

How a gap year can help you academically

• ....

• ....

LINKED SUMMARY

Using the ideas in your notes, write a paragraph of no more than 70 words explaining what benefits you can get from a gap year. Use your own words as far as possible.

General notes from a personal text

EXAMINER'S TIP

Sometimes exam texts are chosen which tell a story from one person's point of view. In this text, for example, Robert explains what happened when he decided to take a gap year. The question asks you to present the information for a general audience, however, so you should use either the second person 'you' or a neutral voice. Do not use 'I' in your notes.

Of course, notes don't have to be in full sentences, so it may not be necessary to use either pronoun. The main point to remember is that your notes have to be clear and make sense, so think carefully about the intended audience for them.

Read the article about a boy who joined the circus. Write a summary outlining why Alex wanted to become a clown, and how his life has changed since he began training as a clown. Write about 100 words and use your own words as far as possible.

From Schoolboy to Clown

Alex Santas, 13, has always had a burning ambition to become a circus clown. A few years ago, his dream started to come true when, accompanied by his parents, he left home to begin training with the circus. 'When Alex was only three,' says his mother Anna, 'we took him to the circus and he absolutely could not take his eyes off the clowns.' Alex still remembers that visit: "I just loved the way the audience was looking and smiling at the clowns. If a juggler drops his clubs, or a trapeze artist falls, it messes up the act. But if a clown falls over, everyone thinks it's a great joke and roars with laughter.'

'Alex was so intrigued by the special power that the clowns seemed to have, he kept asking to visit the circus again,' recalls his father. 'At family parties he used to dress up as a clown and put on a performance doing juggling, comedy routines and magic tricks. Over the years, Alex's love of the circus began to affect the way Anna and I felt. His aspirations were rubbing off on us. Then, unexpectedly, I was made redundant from my job as a gas-heating designer. I was offered similar work with an agency, but Anna and I wanted to explore our dream, so we wrote away to the circus to see if there were any jobs.'

'Eventually David and I were offered jobs with the Moscow State Circus', explains Anna. 'It was so exciting. David worked as a spotlight operator and I worked in the box office, selling tickets. Most important of all, Alex had a chance to begin his training as a clown.'

However, Anna admits that there was a lot of soul-searching and agonising decision-making to do before they finally made up their minds. 'After all,' she says, 'we were leaving our pleasant, centrally-heated house with all its home comforts to live in a small caravan. But Alex was so thrilled at the prospect, and he seemed to have so much talent and flair, we thought, why not?'

After two years, the family joined Zippo's Circus. 'We now go touring, which is marvellous', smiles Anna, 'and David has been promoted to foyer operations manager.'

Although he is not old enough to perform in the circus yet, Alex is continuing to develop his clowning skills. 'I think this way of life is fantastic,' he says. 'and it's even better now that I'm allowed to go out with Dad to perform in front of school audiences when we're on tour.

'People ask about my education,' adds Alex, 'but wherever we are on tour, Mum organises a private tutor to come and teach me. I follow the same books as children at school and I've got a laptop. I just have to make sure I don't fall behind. I've got used to one-to-one teaching and really like it.'

And the future? 'I'm going to be a main clown in a circus one day,' declares Alex firmly.

....

....

....

....

....

....

....

....

....

....

....

....

....

....

....

Developing imaginative skills

This text focuses on a family's dreams and unconventional lifestyle. Even if you have never been to a circus or thought about circuses before, try to use your imagination to project yourself into the situation, to understand what is special and appealing about it. Even though it may not appeal to you personally, ask yourself why someone might be attracted to the circus way of life.

Developing your imaginative skills in this way will not only help you in exams, when reading about unfamiliar situations. It will also enable you to be more adaptable and to relate better to people in all aspects of your life.

Read the article about the way people feel about the development of wind turbines close to their homes. Then make **two** short notes under each of the headings given.

THE *UGLY* SIDE OF CLEAN POWER

The noise, says Les Nichols, is a low thump-thump-thump that reverberates up to 22 times a minute. 'It's not there all the time, but you're always waiting for it,' he says. 'It's a form of torture.'

Les lives besides a wind farm in Furness, a scenic area in the north-west of England. For the past three-and-a-half years, he and his neighbours have had to put up with a level of noise that disrupts their sleep and causes constant stress.

'When the developers sought permission for the seven giant turbines in this area, they guaranteed there would be no noise nuisance or disturbing sounds,' he says. The wind farm is managed by Wind Prospect on behalf of its owner, PowerGen. Bruce Allen, a director of Wind Prospect, said that the fact that no action had been taken to close the wind farm suggested it had not breached planning regulations. He added: 'The noise is a subjective thing – like living next to a busy road.' PowerGen says that it has installed special noise reduction software to eliminate the nuisance.

The government has plans to double the number of wind farms in an effort to derive 20 per cent of electricity from renewable sources. Once regarded as a novelty, wind farms are soaring in popularity as power companies take advantage of generous government subsidies and apply to build turbines on windy sites.

Wind power also receives strong support from environmental groups such as Greenpeace and Friends of the Earth, which believe the cost to the countryside in noise and disfigured landscapes is worth paying for the benefit of reduced air pollution and lower carbon emissions.

Residents, however, argue that having a series of giant wind turbines erected near their homes transforms a tranquil neighbourhood into an ugly and menacing industrial site. At the very least the farms – usually sited along the skyline to benefit from maximum wind – are an eyesore.

Among the other unpleasant effects documented by residents' opposition groups are increased stress from noise vibration and many more visits to the doctor. Angela Kelly, who chairs the anti-wind farm residents' campaign group, Country Guardian, claims they make people ill.

Although wind farms are usually in sparsely-populated rural areas, there are no fixed rules about how near they can be to homes. Government advisers recommend they shouldn't be less that 1.5 kilometres from any house, but developers go as close as between 500 metres and 600 metres. Although Country Guardian have helped to stop the building of many proposed turbines in the past decade, they say the pressure to build more turbines is steadily increasing.

Scotland, for example, has 120 potential wind power sites under consideration. A map produced by concerned residents shows that once the 'zone of visual influence' for each wind farm is drawn in, large areas of Scotland's horizon, coastline and countryside will never again escape the sight of the giant turbines.

Anti-wind farm pressure groups claim that the tiny amount of electricity they produce is not worth the environmental cost. And because the wind itself is unreliable, conventional power stations must be on standby in case they are needed.

The advantages of wind turbines, according to the government and environmental groups

• ....

• ....

Residents' views about the effects of turbines on the environment

• ....

• ....

Effects of turbines on residents' health

• ....

• ....

Why opposition groups think the turbines lack practical value

• ....

• ....

LINKED SUMMARY

Using the ideas in your notes, write a paragraph of no more than 70 words on the pros and cons of wind turbines. Use your own words as far as possible.

Generalising from factual information

Factual items about the impact on modern technology on people's lives are quite popular exam topics. In this case, the wind-power technology is British-based, but the underlying ideas, including why the technology is developing and how it might affect people and the environment, are applicable to many different situations and parts of the world.

It is useful when you are reading a text to think about the ideas in general, rather than only the particular situation described in the text. It is also helpful to think about how your own environment would be altered should these changes happen in your area, as this can help you to understand the implications.

Read the article about Daphne and her experience of family meals. Then write a summary of about 100 words explaining why mealtimes with her own children are usually tense. You should use your own words as far as possible.

What's for dinner, Mum?

I'm the product of a Latin family. That means I was raised in an environment in which food was a vital part of family life and family mealtimes were sacred. The scene around our kitchen table when I was a child must have seemed a bit like a television commercial for the perfect family. I remember us all sitting down to dinner every night, laughing and talking while we consumed huge platefuls of my mum's delicious home cooking.

Actually, when I was younger I sometimes thought my Spanish family was too rigid and insistent about being at home for meals. When I was at college, for example, living miles from home, I used to have to trail home every weekend for Sunday lunch. Although this wasn't always convenient, if I didn't turn up I ran the risk of my strict father cutting me off without my inheritance! Our lives were ruled by the idea that families who eat together, stay together and there were certain expectations regarding eating and mealtimes. In my family, no one ever ate in front of the TV or said, 'I'll grab a sandwich later.'

It's strange that, although I felt resentment about these rules when I was a teenager, now, as a mother of two children myself, I've found that the old habits have reasserted themselves. Now I myself insist that we all sit down together every evening and eat dinner – although frankly, I often wonder why I do this. I have to admit that our mealtimes are rarely civilised affairs, where people smile warmly, compliment the cook and enquire politely about each other's day.

Family meals in our house usually start with a row between 11-year-old Frankie and 14-year-old Jessica about whose turn it is to lay the table, or why one of them has got a drink for themselves, but not for the other. Then, when dinner is served, the annoying grumbles about the food begin – of the 'I hate soup / salad / anything healthy whatsoever' variety. 'Yuk!' said Frankie the other night as I put a dish of lovely home-cooked vegetables on the table, 'I'd really like to shoot that broccoli.'

Mealtimes also seem to lead to quarrels about other things.

Perhaps it's because we're tired and argumentative after a long day at work or school, and sitting down together as a family stirs up conflicts. However much we try, my husband and I can't seem to avoid using this opportunity for telling the children off about the state of their bedrooms, their disregard for the value of money, or their flagrant laziness. Other families, in my imagination, are spending mealtimes having intelligent discussions – about the state of the environment, perhaps. We, meanwhile, are declaring World War Three at our own dinner table.

Don't ask me why my family mealtimes are so confrontational – ask a psychiatrist. Whatever the reason – too much eye contact perhaps? – I do know that I end up feeling very resentful about the time I've spent preparing a tasty meal, only for it to stick in my throat while my family bicker with each other.

Maybe the kids are right after all, and it's time to hang up my apron, put away the saucepans and the cookery books, pick up the 'dial a pizza' menu and let it go.

....
....
....
....
....
....
....
....
....
....
....
....
....
....
....
....
....

Becoming familiar with colloquial style

EXAMINER'S TIP

Chatty items like this article from a family magazine are less common in the exam than more factual pieces. However, they are sometimes used, so it is worth familiarising yourself with their style and approach. They tend to be more light-hearted and humorous, partly because there is often some exaggeration by the author to get a comic effect. The articles also tend to be targeted at a specific audience – in this case other mothers – so there are assumptions about shared experience. This experience may not necessarily reflect your own views or lifestyle, so you may need to think about the ideas carefully and discuss them with your friends.

It is also useful, in general, to broaden your knowledge of colloquial language such as *let it go* or *stick in my throat*, as this will help you become more fluent in English and more able to use a variety of both formal and informal registers. If you take the time occasionally to read magazines in English or watch films, you will also extend your range of conversational English.

Read the article about the growing popularity of modern Indian dance (Bollywood dance). Then write **two** short notes under each of the headings given.

Bolly Girls

It is the highlight of the week for Vishali Sharma, nine, and her sister Roshni, 16. They've changed out of their school uniforms into colourful shalwar kameez costumes for their regular class in modern Indian dance, just as the Bollywood film stars in India do it. I asked them why they enjoyed their classes so much. 'It's easy to learn, the songs are great, and it's got cool, funky movements,' replies Vishali enthusiastically. 'It's more graceful than jazz or street dance.'

Their teacher is dancer and choreographer Honey Kalaria, who leads the teaching of the genre in Britain. Honey launched her dance academy in 1997 from her father's garage in Essex with just four students. Since then, the academy has mushroomed, with more than 800 students taught by 12 teachers in classes and workshops. But the indefatigable Ms Kalria has not stopped there. She is searching for teachers from India with the aim of extending the academy nationwide.

'Dance has huge potential for educating children,' she says. 'The Asian kids love it because it's something they know; and it has so much energy that the non-Asian kids get interested.' She believes that within half an hour, children 'have learned much, and in a way they will remember.'

Her immediate plans involve putting modern Indian dance on a secure educational footing with a national syllabus and public exams. 'Even salsa has its own syllabus and exams,' she says. At present she uses a system of assessment she has devised herself, videotaping her pupils and marking their performance in terms of confidence, style, grace and interpretation.

Modern Indian dance is performed to upbeat, vibrant music, usually hits from Indian movies produced in Mumbai (formerly Bombay). The films, which feature extravagant song and dance numbers, have a huge following around Asia, and wherever Indian culture has taken root.

'Bollywood' dance contains elements of Indian classical dance, exuberant bhangra (the Punjabi harvest dance, widely performed at weddings), more sedate Indian folk dance, disco, jazz and even Latin. It is energetic yet graceful, with every part of the body in motion. 'Bollywood dancers are incredibly versatile. If they are taught well, they should be able to dance to any kind of music,' says Honey, who is starring in a soon-to-be-released Bollywood blockbuster film.

Honey came to Britain with her parents from East Africa, aged four. She started dancing with her mother, imitating Bollywood styles, and won her first dancing prize at the age of 11. In her teens she went to India every summer, taking classes in classical and folk dance. By 13, she had her first paid dancing role, and by 15 she was dancing professionally. 'During the week I was at school, and at weekends I'd be off to Spain, the United States or Scandinavia for performances.'

Her degree in accountancy and public relations has given her sound business sense. 'Five years ago, when I set up the academy, no-one knew what Bollywood was. Now, modern Indian dance is mushrooming. In the next few years it will be everywhere. Everyone is attracted to it,' she says.

Students' opinion of modern Indian dance

• ....

• ....

Honey's aims for developing modern Indian dance

• ....

• ....

Characteristics of modern Indian dance

• ....

• ....

Honey's teenage dancing achievements

• ....

• ....

LINKED SUMMARY

Using the ideas in your notes, write a paragraph of no more than 70 words explaining the nature of modern Indian dance and why students enjoy learning it. Use your own words as far as possible.

Practising with a friend

EXAMINER'S TIP

Have you thought about practising exam-style exercises with a friend? Studying with a friend who is also taking the exam is more motivating than working alone and, because students sometimes put off studying, being together can help you to get down to the hard work of revising.

If you are practising your note-taking and summarising skills, you can try the same exercise together. When you have finished, check each other's work and see what differences there are. Have either of you made any silly mistakes, such as copying words from the text incorrectly? You could also discuss whether you have found the relevant points from the text and consider what improvements could be made to each of your answers.

Read the article about research into modern educational methods. Then write a summary of about 100 words explaining what classroom learning methods were found to be most popular with school students. Try to use your own words as far as possible.

Pupils find internet 'a poor learning tool'

Schoolchildren believe they learn more from traditional methods, such as taking notes from the teacher, than they do from using the internet or watching videos, a government-funded study shows.

The findings will undermine the current trend to put information technology at the heart of learning. The present fashion is to put more and more of the curriculum online and to enable more schools to have faster access to the internet.

The government-funded survey, designed by pupils and carried out by the Science Museum, found that almost half of pupils thought that taking notes from the teacher was one of the most useful classroom activities.

Three-quarters of students said that watching videos was enjoyable but only a quarter of them thought it was effective. Fewer than one in ten rated the internet as useful. The report concluded that: 'The internet, though moderately enjoyable, is ranked very poorly as a learning tool.'

Research commissioned by the Association of Maintained Girls' Schools recently reported similar results. Academics at London Metropolitan University found that the 203 pupils questioned from eight schools valued contact with the teacher most highly. Fewer than a third of pupils said that learning through specially designed science and history computer courses was effective, compared with 70 per cent who said that opportunities to do practical work and listen to teacher explanations were essential.

At Kendrick Girls, a high-performing state school, computers are dotted around the school and pupils spend an hour a week learning how to master information and communications technology (ICT). Pupils, however, regard the internet's use across the curriculum as limited.

India Dhillon, 12, said: 'As I see it, the internet can be quite good but anyone can put anything on it, so you should not necessarily believe what you read. I learn most from listening and writing things down. Answering questions the teacher writes on the board is a good way to remember as well.' Jessica Burns, a classmate, valued textbooks specially written for her age group. Quyen Hoang, 15, a pupil at King Edward V1 school in Birmingham, said that material from the internet was often too easy or complex to be useful.

Children now use computers and the internet in every subject and from an early age. Groups of pupils gathered around a terminal looking at a monitor is a common sight in many classrooms. However, pupils complain that group work such as this can lead to some students not concentrating, distracting others, and generally 'messing around'.

Most headteachers think that there is a place for computers in the classroom but believe the teacher remains the most important resource. Lynn Gadd, the head of Copthall Girls' School in North London, said: 'In my opinion, you cannot just stick pupils in front of a computer and expect learning to happen by itself.'

Some critics also claim that multimedia approaches, including distance learning, e-learning, CD-ROMs and video, are being promoted as a solution to teacher shortages in the mistaken belief that students can access these resources independently and fewer teachers are required.

The Education Minister is not convinced by the criticisms. He argues that computers help teachers to be creative and engage pupils. 'Some people have contested the value of ICT in teaching and learning. I challenge that view.'

....

....

....

....

....

....

....

....

....

....

....

....

....

....

People named in a text

EXAMINER'S TIP

When writing a summary, you often need to use information that was given by a particular person named in the original text. Sometimes the person's name is given and also their job title, nationality and maybe the organisation they work for. Referring to the status of the person is usually not necessary in a summary and uses up a lot of valuable words. Instead you should, if you can, extract only the key information that the person gives. Avoid giving exact quotes from a person's speech. It is better to try to put what they have said in your own words, as briefly as possible.

Read the article about facial transplants and complete the notes under the headings given.

COMPLETE FACIAL TRANSPLANTS POSSIBLE IN NEAR FUTURE

A dramatic new type of transplant – which would see a donor's face grafted onto a recipient – received a cautious welcome yesterday as a surgeon revealed that such an operation could be medically possible shortly.

Experts in medical ethics and a potential recipient applauded the procedure as a means of significantly improving the quality of life of the seriously disfigured patients for whom it is designed.

But a psychologist warned that the Brave New World technology – itself the subject of the Hollywood film 'Face Off' – could be misappropriated for aesthetic and cosmetic reasons, and opens up 'uncharted territory' where the consequences are unknown.

The possibility of the first full-face transplants was raised by Peter Butler, a leading plastic surgeon at the Royal Free Hospital in North London, at a conference of the British Association of Plastic Surgeons yesterday. He stressed it was essential that a moral and ethical debate took place before anyone underwent the operation.

'The technical part is complex but I don't think that's the thing that's going to be the great difficulty. It's the ethical and moral debate that's going to have to take place before the transplants go ahead,' he said.

'A facial transplant is like any other organ transplant because you can actually do it and achieve it with modern immuno-suppression drugs. But it is different because our faces are part of our expression. The face has an emotional function,' he told a BBC news programme.

The microsurgical procedure – already used to transplant skin from one hand to another – would involve the patient's face, facial muscles, skin and subcutaneous fat being removed and being replaced with those of someone who had recently died. Donated blood vessels, arteries and veins would have to be connected to the patient's vessels, with microscopic stitches, along with the nerves.

This method – creating a so-called skin-envelope – would see the patient gaining the skin tone and texture, eyebrow colour and eyelids of their donor, but retaining his or her own bone structure and still looking more like themselves than their donor.

The surgeon predicted that the techniques could be in place in the near future and said there are likely to be just 10-15 severely disfigured people in Britain who could benefit. The procedure could greatly improve the quality of life of people born with facial abnormalities or those disfigured in accidents.

However, a Department of Health spokeswoman stressed that, before this could occur, the procedure would have to be examined by an advisory committee of the National Institute for Clinical Excellence. After this, the Department of Health might launch a consultation process, which was welcomed by the British Medical Association.

Dr Vivienne Nathanson, chairwoman of its ethics committee, said 'There are obviously issues concerning the family of the dead person: how will they feel, knowing someone has the facial characteristics of their loved one? And how will the recipient feel? How we look is very much part of our identity.'

Dr Aric Sigman, a psychologist who has conducted research into facial recognition, predicted that the development would come about because it would ultimately be seen as a way of helping those in great need, but warned it could be abused. 'Inevitably, there will always be people who want to use new medical technology for aesthetic reasons – just to look more attractive, for example. But that shouldn't stop us going ahead with the procedures.' He added that it was difficult to assess the psychological impact. 'This really is uncharted, unexplored territory. It's about a profound identity change.'

Reasons for using the technique

• ....

• ....

Moral and ethical concerns

• ....

• ....

• ....

• ....

• ....

• ....

LINKED SUMMARY

Using the ideas in your notes, write a paragraph of no more than 70 words explaining the objections people might have to facial transplants. Use your own words as far as possible.

Controversial and emotive issues

This article is based on a controversial idea – that of face transplants. It is controversial because people might disagree strongly about the principle of taking surgery to these lengths. Some people might think this surgery crosses a human boundary which should not be crossed. It is also an emotive issue as readers may find the ideas disturbing, distressing and distasteful.

The surgery raises 'moral and ethical concerns' – involving questions of right and wrong. However, the style of writing in the article is not sensational or emotional in tone – issues which are emotive and controversial are not necessarily discussed in that way. The tone is quite neutral and sounds objective. To help you identify the 'moral and ethical' concerns required for the answer, look at some strong key words such as *warned*, *issues* and *abused*. These words are clues which can help you to understand the seriousness of the ideas being discussed.

Read the article about the decline in minority languages. Then write a summary explaining what measurement experts use to assess whether a language is in danger of being lost, and why the students interviewed want to preserve their traditional languages. You should write about 100 words and use your own words as far as possible.

LOST FOR WORDS

A Sami woman in traditional dress

The Scottish island of Lewis, in a remote part of the British Isles, has two languages: English and the local language of Gaelic. In the village post office of Skigersta, little is spoken that isn't in Gaelic. There's Gaelic gossip and Gaelic small talk, and even the business is transacted in Gaelic – a sweet and lilting Celtic tongue.

But while older residents cling to Gaelic, each of the greeting cards in the post office is in English. 'Happy Anniversary' they shout and 'Well done! You've passed your exams!' For Gaelic is an endangered language, constantly threatened by English. Jayne, the 19-year-old daughter of the postmistress, says: 'Gaelic is definitely dying out. It seems to have an image problem among the youth and it's considered uncool and old-fashioned to speak it.'

Jayne, unlike many of her peers, has chosen to remain on Lewis and study for a BA in Gaelic language and culture. In her spare time, she organises traditional dancing classes, and she has taken part in a project to record the memories of older residents. She also hosts a radio programme in Gaelic.

In all of this, her inspiration comes from her grandmother, whose wealth of memories fascinates and motivates her. This close contact with the past has made Jayne realise how much will be lost if Gaelic dies out. 'It is so expressive,' she says. 'There are sayings and phrases that just can't be translated into English. But it's not just that. The language and culture go hand in hand and it makes me sad to see them slipping away. It's part of my roots – part of my ancestry.'

Unesco estimates the degree to which languages are under threat by looking at trends in language use. If 30 per cent of the children in a community no longer learn a language, then experts reckon it to be endangered. Around 3000 languages across the globe – half the world's languages – are thought to be in peril.

One of these is Sami. For thousands of years the Sami people were nomads whose way of life was based on reindeer husbandry around the Arctic Circle. Today, 80,000 Sami live in the extreme north of Europe, where their former herding grounds are divided between Norway, Sweden, Finland and Russia. Many modern Sami have rejected the old language in order to be progressive. This attitude appals 18-year-old Anna Karrstedt. She is at high school, and lives with her family in the Kiruna region of Sweden.

Where Jayne regards Gaelic as her first language, so Anna regards Sami as her mother tongue. Her enthusiasm for her ancestry and cultural heritage is also inspired by her grandmother, who has taught her many of the old skills associated with reindeer tending.

'I get so much joy out of being Sami and using the language,' she says. 'I feel my Sami life is like an extra life. I would be so sad to see my language die out. I have my Swedish friends, but at the weekends I go off to the mountains with my uncle and get to be with the reindeer and with nature.'

These days few young Sami or teenagers on Lewis expect to survive using the traditional skills, but both Jayne and Anna are determined to preserve their heritage. 'If there aren't any reindeer when my grandchildren are born, I would at least like to tell them how it was for me and my grandmother', says Anna. 'And, most of all, I would like to pass on the language.'

....

....

....

....

....

....

....

....

....

....

....

....

....

....

....

Analysing correct answers

EXAMINER'S TIP

Students sometimes say they feel rather disappointed with the marks they get for their practice notes and summaries, as they have been given lower marks than they were hoping for. They feel that they tackled the questions well and assumed they would get the highest marks. Often students are very close to the answer required, but unfortunately not quite close enough. The reason might be to do with the actual content chosen, or the way they have phrased their answers.

One way to see the difference between your own answer and the correct answer is to look at the corrections your teacher makes when giving work back. Another is to go through the right answers together in class and correct your own work. Whichever method you use, take a bit of time to study the differences between the correct answers and your own answers carefully, because often it is small changes which make the difference. You can also discuss with a friend the way you have worded your answers and compare notes. This is a good way to get further understanding of the phrasing or choices of content you have made.

Read the article about ways to manage water supplies in the future and complete the notes under the headings given.

Thirsty Work

More than 70 per cent of the world is covered with water in seas and oceans. The fact is, though, that 97 per cent of water is too salty for use, and most of the fresh water in the world is too difficult to reach. Much of it is underground or frozen in icebergs. Only one per cent of the earth's fresh water is readily available, but that, if managed properly, is plenty to meet the world's needs.

However, even this one per cent is sometimes unsafe to drink. Every day, 14,000 people die because their water is polluted by dangerous chemicals or untreated sewage. Diarrhoea, caused by dirty water and dirty conditions, kills more than one million children a year through dehydration. Hundreds of millions of people suffer repeated bouts of diarrhoea which does not kill them but saps their energy and ability to work and grow food.

Governments are increasingly recognising that their nation's health is dependent on sanitation. The most successful schemes focus on involving a town or village in developing a supply of clean drinking water. Wells are often the best solution for a long-term, sustainable water supply.

The whole community is encouraged to take part in the planning and building of the well. The well is then maintained, mended and generally taken care of by local people without the need for outside help. The water pump, for example, sometimes breaks, but it can soon be fixed, as the community has been trained in doing repairs with inexpensive, easily available tools.

The schemes also aim to educate people about the need to avoid washing in contaminated water into which waste has been pumped. Where these schemes have been implemented, the well-being of the whole community has improved dramatically.

In addition to finding solutions to the problems of clean drinking water, experts are also considering ways to reduce the impact of water shortages on the world's food production. Already 40 per cent of the world's population lives in countries where water is scarce. By 2030, one in five developing countries will be suffering from a water shortage. However, new agricultural techniques are being developed which can increase food production while using little water. By using better seeds and boosting soil fertility with the use of fertilisers, farmers can produce higher yields, obtaining the greatest gains from precious water supplies.

People's attitudes to water vary tremendously, according to the situation in which they live. In some regions, people have to manage with just one bucketful of water for a whole day. This means water for drinking, washing and cooking. On the other hand, in areas where people have a continuous supply of running water, they often use water wastefully and the concept of conserving water is a new one. For example, leaving the tap running while you brush your teeth uses 10 litres of water – the equivalent of a whole day's supply for some people.

Apart from developing better water management policies, many governments are now committed to awareness-raising campaigns, educating both adults and school children about responsible water use. The key to a future in which there is enough water for us all is a simple one: our water needs to be managed wisely, we all need to be careful with it, and we need to start today.

Why wells are a good way of providing a clean water supply

- ....
- ....
- ....
- ....

Ways of increasing food production where there is a water shortage

- ....
- ....

How education can help

- ....
- ....

LINKED SUMMARY

Using the ideas in your notes, write a paragraph of no more than 70 words explaining the advantages of wells in bringing clean water to people. Use your own words as far as possible.

Likely exam topics

EXAMINER'S TIP

Sometimes students ask to be given a list of topics which might come up in the exam, so that they can prepare for them. As this is an English language exam, there is no strictly prescribed topical content. The best advice is to take a wide interest in topics of all kinds.

However, environmental topics, such as those to do with waste and recycling, the effects of global warming, pollution, disappearing wildlife, heat and drought, and other world problems regularly make their appearance in the exam. The reason for using these kinds of topics is because they are of general interest, they are international in perspective, and they affect everyone. They also might involve issues you will be discussing in other parts of your curriculum, such as science or geography.

To help yourself feel more confident and comfortable with the topics, you could watch interesting documentaries, read newspaper features or listen to lively current affairs programmes on the radio in English or your own language. You might find that, not only do you feel more at ease with exam topics, but you also have interesting things to tell your friends after school.

TOPIC VOCABULARY

The topic vocabulary lists on the following pages each relate to one of the 24 texts in the book. Each list is divided into groups of words or phrases of related meaning and can be used in a variety of ways to develop vocabulary awareness.

You can use the lists in whichever way you find helpful, but here are some suggestions:

- label words with their part of speech – noun, verb, adjective, adverb, etc
- write translations next to the items
- write the infinitive of a given verb form
- work out the meaning of an unfamiliar word by looking at the words it is associated with in the same group
- check back in the text to locate the word or phrase and study its context
- give example sentences to illustrate meaning
- think of appropriate headings, e.g. *animals*, *occupations*, *feelings*, for certain word groups
- produce further collocations for a given word
- distinguish differences of meaning between similar words, e.g. between *current* and *tide* or *pat* and *stroke*
- memorise words for spelling tests
- add more words to extend the groups
- use the lists for ideas for a range of possible writing tasks, including work in other areas of the curriculum
- use them to help you with the exam-style writing tasks on pages 82–88.

A doctor in the house *(page 8)*

doctor

dentist

researcher

engineer

expert

therapist

technology

gadget

device

aid

sensor

hi-tech

project

prototype

trial

cancer

melanoma

ulcer

wound

cut

bandage

illness

symptoms

treat

treatment

antibiotics

complications

health

healthy

check-up

doctor's surgery

blood sugar

bacteria

identify

detect

check

monitor

prevent

early warning

Tackling dyslexia in children *(page 10)*

dyslexia

dyslexic

process visual information

eye movement / wobble

focus on

trouble reading and writing

lack of eye control

reading difficulties

the printed page

glare

headache

disturbing sensation

rub your eyes

area of the brain

brain difference

cell

scientist

professor

patient

neurology

clinic

tests

assess

research

connection between

spectacles / specs

mass-produced

adapt

develop

The enemy within (page 12)

allergy

allergic reaction

allergic to

sufferer

food allergy

disorder

asthma

hay fever

trigger a reaction

severe reaction

immune system

virus

parasite

micro-organism

harmless substance

antibody

histamine

chemicals

inflame the tissues

attach itself to

allergen

pollen

nuts

peanuts

strawberries

wasp / bee sting

processed food

additive

colouring

swelling

rash

sneezing

sore eyes

breathlessness

anaphylaxia

lifestyle

double glazing

central heating

find a cure

control symptoms

medicine

avoid contact with

Stop them before they start *(page 14)*

take up smoking

give up / quit smoking

relapse

long-term smoker

nicotine addiction

addicted to cigarettes

hooked

habit

craving

dependent

pleasure

enjoyment

pack of cigarettes

vaccine

vaccinate

booster

effective

stimulate the immune system

antibodies against

prevent

prevention

discourage from

anti-smoking

health problems

at risk

controversial

on the horizon

a long way down the road

Why zoo cats lose their cool (page 16)

big cat

lion

tiger

feline

cub

suspicious

watchful

pace back and forth

pace / move around

prick up their ears

monkey

gorilla

chimpanzee

primate

species

asleep

resting

dozing

yawning

nocturnal

cleaning themselves

licking themselves

grooming

welfare

well-being

health

quality of life

abnormal / strange behaviour

disturbed behaviour

stressed

irritated

zoo keeper

visitor

enclosure

active

vigilant

on the alert

on guard

attract their attention

wave

call

make noise

The thrill of watching whales *(page 18)*

cetaceans

whale

porpoise

dolphin

fin

detect

see

spot

distinguish between

differentiate

sea creature

sea life

marine life

flock of seabirds

wild animal

sighting

pair of binoculars

record details

environmental conditions

distribution

current

tide

wave

break

splash

patient

peaceful

quiet

tranquillity

undisturbed

marine environment

submerged rocks

underwater

land

shore

take your time

sit quietly

The Sabi-Sand game reserve *(page 20)*

game reserve

ranger

tracker

4x4 / four-by-four vehicle

two-way radio

plains

grassland

bush

forest

habitat

elephant

zebra

antelope

leopard

cheetah

wildebeest

buffalo

mammal

predator

purr

markings

rainfall

erosion

drainage

human impact

impact on the environment

co-exist

botany

biology

zoology

astronomy

bushcraft

Dogs on the defensive *(page 22)*

dog	praise
puppy	positive reinforcement
pet	treat
companion	biscuit
hostile	scared
aggressive	frightened
defensive	nervous
growl	agitated
bite	threatened
canine language	trapped
pat	training school
stroke	instructor
handle	trainer
touch	obedient
	difficult to control
	daily walk
fur	
paw	
tail	
owner	
in charge	
command	
obey	

The rose, queen of all flowers (page 24)

grow

cultivate

mass cultivation

agricultural product

favourable climate

hybrid

botanist

flower

bloom

root

stem

leaves

petals

thorns

sharp / prickly

colour

scent

fragrance

rose petals

grain of pollen

preserved / dried flowers

ancient graves / tombs

burial ceremony

appreciated

highly valued

popularity

romantic gift

transportation

lucrative market

all over the world

rose-growing business

symbolise

rich symbolism

A natural antiseptic (page 26)

tea tree oil

tea tree plantation

conifer

bush

bark

needles

spikes

bushy plant

seeds

germinate

seedlings

growing process

transplant

greenhouse / glasshouse

irrigation

watering

pricking-out

weeding

labour intensive

casual labour

distillation process

steam

evaporate

vapour

water-cooled condenser

separator

draw off

fluid

process of extraction

tray

container

bin

drum

stainless steel

pharmacy

health food shop

acne

dry, itchy skin

bruises

burns

dermatitis

fungal infection

antiseptic

antibacterial agent

The mangoes in your trolley (page 28)

wild mangoes

mango tree

mango crop

mango producer

tropical fruit

tropical country

the tropics

temperate climate

global market

lucrative

gain popularity

grow in popularity

high nutritional value

good source of vitamins

protein

fructose

fibre

delicious

sweet, juicy flesh

variable in quality

below the standard required

propagation

select

reject

good quality fruit

best quality seedlings

travel well

air freight / transport

minimum delay

in storage

refrigeration

deteriorate

over-ripe

unfit for sale

supermarket shelves

shoppers

pay extra

at its best

Sweet talk (page 30)

botanical name

chocolate

cocoa tree

cocoa plantation

cocoa bean

cocoa butter

leathery pod

made from

good for the heart

spots

migraine

obesity

stressed-out nerves

irresistible foodstuff

one of the world's favourite foods

crush

boil

add spices

brew

tasty, frothy drink

grind into a powder

heat

sweeten

press into a mould

solid chocolate

bar of chocolate

chocolate truffle

melt

short shelf life

meet the growing demand

more easily available

chemist

food scientist

Young ambassadors (page 32)

go abroad

a year abroad / overseas

a year off

host country / community

overseas university

home university

foreign institution

undergraduate

language student

degree programme

linguistic and cultural immersion

culture shock

untapped reserves

tenacity

fortitude

perseverance

initiative

open-mindedness

curiosity

broaden the mind

gain insights into

responsibilities

obligations

attend lectures

do coursework

complete an assignment

improve academic skills

keep in touch

maintain contact

give support

keep informed

personal tutor

lecturer

briefing

checklist

guide

handbook

web-based information

questionnaire

Lost on the mountain (page 34)

mountain

jungle

dense rainforest

gorge

swamp

stream

waterfall

slope

ridge

rocky gully

thick vegetation

injured

scratched

cut

bruised

unharmed

ordeal

helicopter

search party

in groups of four

armed with walkie-talkies

keep close together

hard to find

out in the open

failure to spot her

infested with

poisonous snakes

vines

tendrils

lacerate bare skin

resourceful

calm

terrified

exhausted

dumbfounded

survive

survival

remarkable escape

weather conditions

unusually warm and dry

clamber over boulders

hack through the undergrowth

loose rocks underfoot

My daughter can achieve whatever she wants *(page 36)*

disability

lost her feet

be fitted with

be measured for

prosthetic limb

artificial leg

cold to the touch

stare

make comments

unkind

teasing

hurt

upset

take to heart

reluctant to take part

give something a go

encourage

make a big difference

activities

sports

swimming

skiing

private treatment

specialist

orthopaedic centre

silicone

realistic-looking

match her exact skin tone

fund-raising event

sponsored event

donation

raffle

confidence

able to do anything

Taking a gap year *(page 38)*

careers information

go to university

exam results

place at university

year out

gap year

trip

foreign expedition

see the world

thousands of miles away

backpacking

mountaineering

trekking

sign up

raise money

fare and expenses

meet the target

skills

personal qualities

daunting

hard work

nerve-wracking

stunning

incredible

inspiring

tolerance

accept other people

consider other people

help each other

make you less selfish

distracted from your studies

concentrate

analyse information

From schoolboy to clown (page 40)

burning ambition

his dream came true

aspirations

love of the circus

thrilled at the prospect

begin training

talent

flair

clown

juggler

juggling

clubs

trapeze artist

perform in front of

audience

clowning skills

dress up as

put on a performance

comedy routine

magic trick

fall over

mess up the act

roar with laughter

be made redundant

be offered work / a job

be promoted

home comforts

caravan

on tour

way of life

private tutor

one-to-one teaching

fall behind

exciting

marvellous

fantastic

agonising

soul-searching

decision-making

The ugly side of clean power *(page 42)*

wind turbine	countryside
wind farm	horizon
wind power	skyline
	coastline
level of noise	
noise nuisance	sparsely populated
vibration	rural area
disturbing sounds	windy site
low thump	disfigured landscape
reverberate	ugly
	eyesore
form of torture	
disrupt your sleep	environmental cost
put up with	environmental group
cause constant stress	campaign group
make people ill	opposition group
	concerned residents
electricity	
renewable sources	breach planning regulations
power company	government subsidies
conventional power station	developer
reduced air pollution	take advantage of
lower carbon emissions	benefit from

What's for dinner, Mum? *(page 44)*

family meals

family mealtimes

family life

sit down to dinner

sit down together as a family

eat together

eat in front of the TV

grab a sandwich

delicious home cooking

huge platefuls

tasty

kitchen table

dinner table

serve dinner

rigid

strict

insist

insistent

expectations

resentment

resentful

row

quarrel

bicker

grumble

tell the children off

confrontational

argumentative

conflict

declare war

lay the table

compliment the cook

civilised

intelligent discussion

enquire politely about

apron

saucepan

cookery book

Bolly girls (page 46)

growing popularity

highlight of the week

film star

blockbuster film

hits from Indian movies

song and dance number

have a huge following

modern Indian dance

folk dance

classical dance

salsa

disco

jazz

street dance

graceful

energetic

exuberant

sedate

versatile

style

grace

interpretation

upbeat, vibrant music

cool, funky movements

dance academy

class

workshop

choreographer

dancer

pupil

costume

national syllabus

public exam

system of assessment

mark their performance

dance professionally

dance to any kind of music

sound business sense

huge potential

the academy has mushroomed

extend the academy nationwide

Pupils find internet 'a poor learning tool' *(page 48)*

traditional method

educational method

learning method

learning tool

current trend

present fashion

information and communications technology (ICT)

multimedia approach

e-learning

CD-ROM

put the curriculum online

access to the internet

important resource

classroom activities

take notes from the teacher

use the internet

watch videos

contact with the teacher

do practical work

listen to explanations

group work

gather around a terminal

look at a monitor

concentrate

distract others

mess around

government-funded survey / study

commission research

report findings / results

pupil

classmate

head teacher

textbook

computer

rate as useful

value highly

rank poorly

effective

moderately enjoyable

Complete facial transplants possible in near future *(page 50)*

facial transplant

organ transplant

donor

recipient

patient

medically possible

undergo an operation

facial abnormality

facial characteristics

seriously disfigured

for aesthetic / cosmetic reasons

look more attractive

psychologist

plastic surgeon

graft

microsurgical procedure

technique

microscopic stitches

immuno-suppression drugs

facial muscles

subcutaneous fat

blood vessels

arteries

veins

nerves

skin tone and texture

bone structure

medical ethics

moral and ethical debate

issues concerning

consultation process

psychological impact

profound identity change

conduct research

new medical technology

go ahead with

uncharted / unexplored territory

unknown consequences

Lost for words *(page 52)*

minority language

local language

endangered

threatened by

under threat

in danger of being lost

in peril

die out

slip away

preserve

cling to

pass on

first language

mother tongue

ancestry

cultural heritage

contact with the past

wealth of memories

older residents

traditional skills

way of life

nomad

gossip

small talk

lilting

expressive

phrase

saying

image problem

old-fashioned

uncool

reject

inspiration

inspire

fascinate

motivate

Thirsty work *(page 54)*

fresh water

water supply

supply of clean drinking water

running water

water shortage

scarce

build a well

maintain

mend / fix

do repairs

dirty water

unsafe to drink

contaminated

polluted

untreated sewage

dangerous chemicals

diarrhoea

dehydration

sanitation

sap your energy

long-term

sustainable

implement a scheme

improve dramatically

water management policies

awareness-raising campaign

responsible water use

conserve water

leave the tap running

bucketful of water

developing country

the whole community

local people

WRITING TASKS

The suggested number of words for each of the following tasks is **100–150** words for Core level and **150–200** words for Extended level.

Writing Task 1 *(see page 57 for related topic vocabulary)*

In your local newspaper you read an article which says that, in future, people will use a computer at the doctor's surgery to find out what is wrong with them and the computer will prescribe a course of treatment. The number of doctors at the surgery will be reduced and some people may find they rarely see a doctor face to face.

Here are some comments made by other readers of the newspaper:

'A good idea – I find talking to a doctor always makes me feel embarrassed.'

'I hate the thought – computerised gadgets can never have the skills of a real doctor.'

'I'm too busy to wait ages at the surgery to see a doctor. This will save time and cost less money.'

'A negative development – when you are ill you need to see a kind, caring professional, not a machine.'

Write a letter to the editor of the newspaper giving *your* views on the issue. The comments above may give you some ideas, but you are free to use any ideas of your own.

Writing Task 2 *(see page 58 for related topic vocabulary)*

STUDENT MAGAZINE COMPETITION

Students! Do you know someone who has overcome a learning problem and gone on to succeed in education? If you do, tell us their story. We have fantastic packages of DVD or book vouchers to give to the three people who most deserve them.

Please send all entries to Nicola, Student Magazine Editor, Room 17 by Thursday.

You decide to enter this competition. In your article for the school magazine, don't forget to say:
• who the person is
• what kind of learning difficulty they had
• how they overcame the learning difficulty
• why you think this person could be a good example to others who have a similar problem.

Writing Task 3 *(see page 59 for related topic vocabulary)*

You were enjoying a special family party when you had an allergic reaction for the first time to something you ate. Write a letter to a friend in which you explain:
• why the party was taking place
• what happened when you had the allergic reaction
• how other people reacted
• what treatment you had, if any
• how you are feeling now.

Writing Task 4 *(see page 60 for related topic vocabulary)*

There are plans to ban cigarette advertising in newspapers and magazines that are aimed at young people. Here are some comments made by your friends:

'The advertising ban would be a good idea as smoking is very addictive and bad for your health.'

'It wouldn't make any difference. Advertising cigarettes doesn't increase the number of young people who smoke.'

'I agree with the ban. Young people are easily influenced. They will smoke if they see it shown as a glamorous thing to do.'

'I'm against the idea. Lots of people are employed in the tobacco industry, and they may lose their jobs if there are fewer smokers.'

Write an article for your local newspaper giving *your* views on the issue. The comments above may give you some ideas, but you are free to use any ideas of your own.

Writing Task 5 *(see page 61 for related topic vocabulary)*

You recently visited a local zoo and were sorry to see large animals appearing restless and unhappy. Write a letter to the zoo manager describing your visit and suggesting some ways the zoo could improve the care of the animals.

Don't forget to include:
• details of when you made the visit
• examples of distress in the animals
• examples of ways some of the visitors were disturbing the animals
• your suggestions for ways the care of the animals could be improved.

Writing Task 6 *(see page 62 for related topic vocabulary)*

You recently enjoyed a holiday by the sea and were lucky enough at times to see some interesting sea life. Write a letter to a friend describing your holiday.

Don't forget to include:
• where you went on holiday
• what you enjoyed about the holiday
• details of the sea life you observed
• why your friend might enjoy a holiday like this too.

Writing Task 7 *(see page 63 for related topic vocabulary)*

Some time ago, you entered a competition and won a safari holiday at a game reserve in Southern Africa. Write a letter to a friend describing your holiday.

Don't forget to include:
• what the game reserve you went to was like

• how you travelled around the reserve and who accompanied you
• details of the wild animals you observed
• a special memory of the holiday
• whether you would recommend a safari holiday to other people.

Writing Task 8 *(see page 64 for related topic vocabulary)*

You have recently acquired a new puppy but unfortunately it has been rather difficult to control. Write a letter to a friend in which you:
• describe your new puppy

• say what you like about having a dog
• explain what you have done to train him/her
• say whether you think you are succeeding in controlling your new dog.

Writing Task 9 *(see page 65 for related topic vocabulary)*

A rich citizen of your town died recently. He left the town a sum of money to improve the town park, and your town council has asked local people to suggest ways this could be done. You think planting a rose garden would be a good idea. Write a letter to your local newspaper giving your views.

Your letter should cover:
• where in the park the rose garden should be planted
• why a rose garden would improve the park
• how local people might use it
• why the rose has always been a special and popular flower.

Writing Task 10 *(see page 66 for related topic vocabulary)*

COMPETITION!

Buzz magazine wants to find our which skin care products its readers use. Let us know about the product you prefer and why, and we'll print the best articles. The lucky winners will also receive a whole basket of skin care products **or** six DVDs and CDs of their choice.

You see this competition in a teenage magazine and decide to submit an entry. In your article you could include:
• why teenage skin can be problematic

• good methods for caring for teenage skin
• which skin care product you use and why
• whether you would recommend this product to other teenagers.

Writing Task 11 *(see page 67 for related topic vocabulary)*

DO YOU LIKE FRUIT?

Our school survey has found that lots of us are not eating enough fruit! If you enjoy fruit, we'd like to hear from you, especially if you like eating more unusual varieties. *All articles to the School Newsletter Editor by **Friday**, please.*

You like fruit and decide to submit an article for the school newsletter explaining why. In your article you should say:
• what kinds of fruit you like eating

• what you look for when you buy fruit
• why fruit is good for you.
• why your friends should try some new kinds of fruit.

Writing Task 12 *(see page 68 for related topic vocabulary)*

> **HEAD TEACHER'S ANNOUNCEMENT**
> Each year we raise money for a charity of the students' choice. Please say which charity you would like to support this year and submit ideas for ways to raise funds. I promise all your ideas will be carefully considered.

Your class has decided it would be fun to get together to make a variety of things from chocolate (cakes, drinks, etc) and to sell them to raise money for charity. Write a letter to your head teacher with your suggestions.

In your letter you should:
• say which charity your class wants to support
• explain when and where the chocolate items will be made and sold
• say why you think the chocolate products will be popular
• estimate how much money the sale will make.

Writing Task 13 *(see page 69 for related topic vocabulary)*

> Lots of young people now spend a year overseas as part of their studies. If you hope to do this, **Cool Kids** would be interested in hearing which country you would like to go to and what you hope to get out of it.

You see this announcement in a teenage magazine and decide to write an article. In your article you should cover:
• why you would like to study abroad
• which country you would like to study in
• how you think you would cope with the challenges
• how you plan to prepare for your year of study abroad
• what you hope to achieve from a year abroad.

Writing Task 14 *(see page 70 for related topic vocabulary)*

On a recent school camping holiday, two of the younger children got lost. You took part in the search party which eventually found them safe and well. Write a letter to a friend describing the experience.

In your letter you should say:
• where you were camping and why
• what happened when everyone realised the children were missing
• what the search party did
• what happened in the end.

Writing Task 15 *(see page 71 for related topic vocabulary)*

On a visit to your local sports centre, you realise very few disabled people use the facilities. You believe the centre could do more to encourage their participation in sports. Write a letter to the sports centre manager expressing these views.

In your letter you should mention:
• the length of time you have been a member

• what you enjoy about using the facilities
• why you think sport is for everyone, regardless of disability
• how the centre could encourage more people with disabilities to join.

Writing Task 16 *(see page 72 for related topic vocabulary)*

Is a 'gap year' between school and university a good idea, or is it a waste of time? Here are some comments made by young people about the concept:

'A gap year helps you grow up and become more mature.'

'You don't achieve anything in a gap year – you just laze around.'

'It's an opportunity to have a break from studying and do something really different.'

'If you travel in a gap year it's very expensive. I'd rather use the money to help with my studies.'

Write an article for the school magazine expressing *your* views on a gap year. The comments above may give you some ideas, but you are free to develop ideas of your own.

Writing Task 17 *(see page 73 for related topic vocabulary)*

You recently visited a circus. Write a letter to a friend describing your visit and saying what you most enjoyed about it.

Your letter should cover:
• why you visited the circus

• the atmosphere and range of performances
• any acts you particularly liked
• whether you would recommend a circus visit to your friend.

Writing Task 18 *(see page 74 for related topic vocabulary)*

There are plans to build a large recycling plant near where you live, to recycle glass, tins and paper. Write a letter to your local newspaper saying whether or not you think this is a good idea.

Here are some comments from your neighbours:

'The recycling plant will provide jobs in our area, which we need.'

'I hate the thought of the noise and the levels of pollution the plant will bring.'

'We all throw too much away – the recycling plant is part of our efforts to protect the environment.'

'The recycling plant is going to look so ugly and spoil an attractive landscape.'

The comments above may give you some ideas, but you are free to use any ideas of your own.

Writing Task 19 *(see page 75 for related topic vocabulary)*

Are family meal times outdated in modern society or are they a tradition worth keeping? Here are some comments made by your classmates:

'We rarely sit down to a family meal as we are so busy with other activities.'

'A family meal makes us feel like a family – I love them.'

'It's not fair to expect mum or dad to make dinner when they've been working all day. We heat up a microwave meal if we're hungry.'

'Dinnertime is an important time when we all meet and share the news of the day.'

Write an article for a teenage magazine giving *your* views on the issue. The comments above may give you some ideas, but you are free to use ideas of your own.

Writing Task 20 *(see page 76 for related topic vocabulary)*

Lots of us find our lunchtimes a bit dull. How about starting some new clubs which would brighten up everyone's day? Please send any ideas for lunchtime clubs to the school newsletter and we will definitely print them!

The above information appears in your school newsletter. You decide to write, suggesting a lunchtime dance club. In your article, don't forget to include:

• what kind of dance club you are suggesting
• where and when in the school you could meet
• why this activity would be popular with students
• who would help organise it.

Writing Task 21 *(see page 77 for related topic vocabulary)*

Your school has been given a large sum of money to spend on improvements. The school is thinking of spending the money on a new computer suite but will consider the views of the students before doing so. Here are some comments from students in your class:

'It's great – we'll be able to use the internet and CD-Roms to help us learn.'

'A bad idea – we need more books and teachers, not computers.'

'We need to develop our computer skills if we are to get good jobs in the future.'

'Let's spend the money on a swimming pool or new sports equipment.'

Write an article for the school magazine giving *your* views on the issue. The comments above may give you some ideas, but you are free to use any ideas of your own.

Writing Task 22 *(see page 78 for related topic vocabulary)*

You have read in your local newspaper that advances in medical science mean that, in future, it may be possible for scientists to alter the genetic make up of an unborn baby. Do you think this is a good idea? Here are some comments from readers of the newspaper about these developments:

'It would be a good way of preventing genetic disorders being passed on through families and this will save so much suffering.'

'I'm concerned about the idea. Parents might ask scientists to help them for the wrong reasons – so they can have a super-intelligent baby, for example, or one who is very beautiful.'

'A good idea. No one wants to have a baby who is not healthy. This enables people to have more control over their lives.'

'I disagree. It's very sad when babies are born with serious conditions but the best attitude is to accept it and care for them.'

Write a letter to the newspaper giving *your* views on the issue. The comments above may give you some ideas, but you are free to use any ideas of your own.

Writing Task 23 *(see page 79 for related topic vocabulary)*

In many countries, more people are speaking English as a second or additional language. Experts believe this trend will increase. How far do you think the spread of the English language is a positive development? Here are some comments made by young people:

'In my view, it's sensible to have a world language such as English because it makes international communication easier.'

'I see it as a negative trend. The spread of English is making other languages less important.'

'I don't mind – we can still use our first language whenever we want to.'

'If people want a good job they think learning English is a priority. Then children don't want to study their own language or literature properly.'

Write an article for your local newspaper giving *your* views about the spread of the English language across the world. The comments above may give you some ideas, but you are free to use any ideas of your own.

Writing Task 24 *(see page 80 for related topic vocabulary)*

You have noticed people in your area being very careless in the way that they use water. You are concerned abut this and decide to write a letter to your local newspaper outlining your views. In your letter, you may wish to include such things as:

- why water is so important
- examples of people wasting water
- problems the lack of clean water can cause
- how we could teach people, especially children, to respect water.